MODERN CULTURE
FROM A
COMPARATIVE
PERSPECTIVE

MODERN CULTURE FROM A COMPARATIVE PERSPECTIVE

༄ঙৃଚ

WILFRED CANTWELL SMITH

Edited by John W. Burbidge

State University
of New York
Press

Published by
State University of New York Press, Albany

© 1997 Wilfred Cantwell Smith and John Burbidge

For information, address State University of New York Press,
State University Plaza, Albany, N.Y., 12246

Production by Marilyn P. Semerad
Marketing by Fran Keneston

Library of Congress Cataloging-in-Publication Data

Smith, Wilfred Cantwell, 1916–
    Modern culture from a comparative perspective / Wilfred Cantwell
Smith ; edited by John W. Burbidge.
        p.   cm.
    Includes bibliographical references (p.   ) and index.
    ISBN 0-7914-3393-5 (hc : alk. paper). — ISBN 0-7914-3394-3 (pb :
alk. paper)
        1. Religion and culture. 2. Civilization, Modern—20th century.
    3. Religion and science. 4. Religion and the humanities.
    5. Religious fundamentalism. 6. Humanism. I. Burbidge, John W.,
    1936–   . II. Title.
    BL65.C8S59 1997
    291.1′75—dc21   96-45432
                                                                CIP

10 9 8 7 6 5 4 3 2 1

CONTENTS

PREFACE

We humans start out as parochial creatures. We accept without question the values and standards of our own culture. And we regard the practices of others not only as strange, but as fundamentally misguided and wrong. Whatever is familiar to us we take to be the norm for all; whoever speaks a different language, eats different food, or worships different gods (indeed any gods at all) has somehow perverted human nature.

Without too much effort we come to the point of comparing others with each other. Some are more perceptive than others; a few, more imaginative and creative. But even then we retain as unquestioned the norms of our own world. Good societies are those that have espoused those values of liberal tolerance and personal well-being we have placed at the centre of our own.

At this stage, seldom, if ever, do we assess our own culture against the standards of others. Seldom, if ever, do we pay attention to the timber in our own eye, for all that we have cavilled at the slivers in the eyes of others.

To surrender our partiality requires a genuinely historical standpoint. It is now conventional wisdom that historians write their accounts from their own ideological perspective. But the study of history can lead to another result. For when we immerse ourselves in the flow of time, in the ebb and flow of cultures, in the immense drama of human life on our planet, we acquire a sense of perspective. Just as the exploration of outer space has offered a vision of our earth as one small planet among many; so the study of history recognizes that our contemporary culture is but one expression of human life within a vast panorama of different communities and societies. Ours is but the most recent and, to us, most familiar.

Even after we have moved to this level of insight, our values can still claim preeminence. For they include a belief in progress, in the gradual evolution from more basic to more developed, from worse to better. Because technology can build on the achievements of the past to produce ever more intricate tools, we presume that the same holds good for the things humans value. The complexity of our modern civilization incorporates all the moral and spiritual achievements of the past with a richness that is better because it is the more comprehensive. Whatever has been lost in the course of human progress has not been worth saving.

The dialectic, however, can nonetheless turn around and invert our values. By enlarging our perspective over a range of cultures, historians have taught us what other cultures value. As we learn that many societies share in affirming virtues which have come to be despised and disregarded within our own, a new approach emerges. In our mind the standards and norms of many different societies enter into dialogue with each other. Each sets a standard for the others; and in due course one's own comes under as much judgement as those which at first appeared strange. As a result, a genuinely comparative approach no longer stands outside of what it studies, but becomes itself one component in the comparison.

Such has been the achievement of Wilfred Cantwell Smith. Starting with a study of Islam, particularly in its dialogue with the modern liberalism of the West, he broadened his field of vision until it incorporated the religious history of humankind. Now he has turned back to the culture within which he functions—not simply to the Protestant Christianity of his upbringing, but also to the academic world of the liberal and humane sciences. The essays collected within this volume capture the results of that reflection.

Central to a culture is its ultimate commitment—what is understood to transcend the finite, limited world within which we all live. This, traditionally, has been called religion. And in the first essay, "Religion as Symbolism", Smith offers not only a way of studying the faith and the commitment of others, but also an approach which can be applied to our own world. The second essay, "History in Relation to both Science and Religion", takes this methodological consideration further, and shows the role the study of history plays in understanding how cultures relate to and with each other.

Using these principles of investigation Smith then turns to look at a "religious" commitment of the Western world that has too often been overlooked. "Philosophia as One of the Religious Traditions of Humankind" shows how the transcendent need not be limited to God, however defined. It may also refer to Truth and Wisdom and Reality; and those who respond make a religious commitment that can transform both self and society. The fourth essay, "On Mistranslated Booktitles", explores through our use of language how the original vision of Philosophia has come to be distorted—how belief in the transcendent has become domesti-cated and secularized.

Secularism denies the transcendent. And it raises questions about the future of faith. So Smith explores the effects of secularism in both this century and the next ("Shall Next Century be Secular or Religious?"). It is at this point that Smith's historical approach comes into play. For secularism claims to be the last (up to now) result of human progressive development. When viewed compara-tively, however, the secular is seen as an exception within a general practice where humans relate themselves to that which is above and beyond themselves. Rather than an enrichment of human cul-ture, it has become an impoverishment—a loss of depth, and a loss of resonance. This loss has provoked the rise of what has been called the new fundamentalism, as Smith points out in "Islamic Resurgence".

Historical and comparative analyses offer not only the oppor-tunity to evaluate the limitations of one's own culture. They may also point toward correctives—ways in which the present can be enriched by learning from others, both in the present and in the past. The modern secular form of Philosophia is no exception. For those who espouse it can learn from the Arabs that truth means more than correctness ("A Human View of Truth"). And they can learn from religious traditions generally that objectivity means rec-ognizing the diversity and richness of the people who are them-selves involved and committed to the quest for transcendence. As Smith argues in "Objectivity and the Humane Sciences", to study humans objectively is to respect them as subjects.

For all that these papers have appeared in various places over several decades, then, they nevertheless develop a single, coherent thesis. From a religious perspective, we must include more within our purview than is frequently assumed. After all, transcendence takes many forms. Indeed our own Western culture has a tradition of transcendence that has usually been excluded from the list of religions. Once it is included, and its more recent perversions recognized, we can prepare for our future in a way that is both more realistic about the total panorama of human culture and more appropriate to the inherent demands of human nature.

By thus opening our eyes to many facets of our own cultural environment, Wilfred Cantwell Smith has helped us transcend our parochial tendencies, and become citizens of the world—a world which includes not only the many cultures of the present, but all the riches of the past as well.

JOHN W. BURBIDGE

ACKNOWLEDGEMENTS

The author and the editor wish to thank the following publishers for their permission to reprint copyright material originally published elsewhere:

Encyclopaedia Britannica, Inc. for 'Religion as Symbolism', reprinted with permission from the Propaedia of *Encyclopaedia Britannica*, 15th edition, © 1974 by Encyclopaedia Britannica, Inc.; Scottish Journal of Religious Studies for 'History in Relation to Both Science and Religion', *Scottish Journal of Religious Studies* (1981) 2: 3–10; Éditions de l'École des Hautes Études en Sciences Sociales for 'Philosophia, as One of the Religious Traditions of Humankind: The Greek Legacy in Western Civilization, viewed by a Comparativist', in *Différences, valeurs, hiérarchie: Textes offerts à Louis Dumont*, edited by Jean-Claude Galey (Paris, 1984), 253–79, © École des Hautes Études en Sciences Sociales; Cambridge University Press for permission to reprint 'On Mistranslated Booktitles', *Religious Studies* (1984) 20: 27–42; Tenri Yamato Culture Congress for 'Shall the Next Century be Secular or Religious?' in Tenri International Symposium '86: *Cosmos, Life, Religion: Beyond Humanism* (Tenri, Japan: Tenri University Press, [1988]), 125–51; the Canadian Corporation for Studies in Religion for 'A Human View of Truth', *Studies in Religion/Sciences Religieuses* (1971) 1, 1: 6–24, (reprinted in *Truth and Dialogue: The Relationship between World Religions*, edited by John Hick [London: Sheldon Press, 1974] and *Truth and Dialogue in World Religions: Conflicting Truth Claims* [Philadelphia: Westminster Press, 1974], 20–44); the Royal Society of Canada for 'Objectivity and the Humane Sciences: A New Proposal', *Transactions of the Royal Society of Canada*, Series 4, 12: 81–102, (reprinted in *Symposium on the Frontiers and Limitations of Knowledge / Colloque sur les frontières et limites du savoir*, edited Claude Fortier, et al. [Ottawa: Royal Society of Canada, 1974], and as Chapter 9 in *Religious Diversity: Essays by Wilfred Cantwell Smith*, edited by

Willard G. Oxtoby [New York: Harper and Row, 1976 and New York: Crossroad, 1982]). 'Islamic Resurgence' is also appearing in *Consciousness and Reality—in memory of Toshihiko Izutsu* (Japan: Iwanami, 1997).

In preparing this volume for publication, Dr. Smith initiated all substantial changes in wording from the original papers; he also has preserved certain British–and–Canadian spellings and styles in place of more conventional American—and is grateful to SUNY for accepting this. The editor provided cross references to other papers in this volume and collected common citations into a single list at the end.

CHAPTER 1

Religion as Symbolism

There is more to human life than meets the eye. More to oneself; more to one's neighbour; more to the world that surrounds us. There is more to the past out of which we come; and especially, it would seem, more to the present moment, maybe even infinitely more. There is more to the interrelationships that bind us together as persons. And the further we probe, people have always found, the deeper the mystery, or the reward, or the involvement. It is this 'more', perhaps, that provides at least one of the bases for human religion. We humans have seldom been content to be 'superficial', to remain on the surface, to imagine that reality does not transcend our finite grasp; and throughout most of our history on this planet we have ordered our lives, both personal and cultural, in terms of that transcendence.

Yet how is one to point to what one does not visually see? How to resort to a milieu beyond all space? How to talk or to think about what transcends not only words but the reach of the mind? How even to feel about what one does not touch? Our inherent and characteristic capacity to do these things finds expression through our special relation to symbols. These have proven over the centuries sometimes more, sometimes less, adequate to such a task, but in any case indispensable, and ubiquitous. Such symbols, it turns out, have the power not merely to express our otherwise inchoate awareness of the richness of what lies under the surface, but also to nurture and to communicate and to elicit it. They have an activating as well as a representational quality, and an ability to organize the emotions and the unconscious as well as the conscious mind, so that into them we may pour the deepest range of our humanity and from them derive an enhancement of the personality. Without the use of symbols, including religious symbols, we would be radically less than human.

Quite diverse types of things have served the purpose: a beaver, the sky, a ceremonial procedure, silence; erotic love, or austere asceticism; the Qur'an; an historical figure; reason. The variety has been immense, different groups having chosen different things to serve them as symbols, not all equally successful. Virtually universal, however, is that people have found it possible to designate some item from within the visible world and to sacralize it in such a way that it becomes then for them the symbol or locus of the invisible, the transcendent. In Japan, a simple open gateway (*torii*) marks off the shrine precincts: one passes through it, leaving behind psychologically, symbolically, the humdrum ordinary world to enter the sacred space of the temple; and after worship, one again moves through the gate in the other direction, to re-enter now the realm of everyday life, but as a renewed person. Virtually all peoples have set aside some portion of what outsiders would regard as ordinary terrain to serve for them as sacred space, erecting in it temple, church, or shrine whereby is then represented for them, often with great force, quite another dimension of reality.

Similarly with time: Jews, for instance, set apart one day in seven, whereby the other six days symbolize the mundane world with its bitter imperfections, perhaps its devastating pain, and at best its transient successes, while the Sabbath creatively represents the inviolate splendour of transcendence—with which therefore the other six days, however bleak, cannot keep them out of touch. Every people has its festivals, weekly or seasonal or occasional, its sacred times when life in its empirical and work-a-day aspects is transcended and life in its timeless dimension is reaffirmed, reactivated: moments when truth, significance, worth are recognized and cultivated—and carried back then into the ordinary world.

We are somehow aware, if only through imaginative vision or sensibility or our special capacity for hope, not only of what is but also of what ought to be. We have sensed that the *status quo* (nowadays, the *fluxus quo*) is not the final truth about humans or the world. We have felt, to take one example, that social justice and concord, personal righteousness, health and joy stand over against the current observable condition of strife, loneliness, wickedness, poverty, and sorrow not as fancy against truth, wishful and irrational dreaming against reality, but in some fashion *vice versa*—as a norm by which the present imperfect world is judged, in some sense a truth in relation to which empirical actuality is in some sense an error. This too has been affirmed symbolically. One rather common way of doing so has been by representing a more perfect world elsewhere. Some have located their utopias chronologically in the past ('Once upon a time'; or Golden Age theories, as in Greece and India); or in the future (millennialisms, a coming just ruler, secular ideas of progress, a life after death); or geographically, somewhere else (the medieval Irish 'Isle of the Blessed' in the then inaccessible Western Sea); or high above the sky (heaven, the heaven of heavens); or in a domain beyond time (Paradise); or in another realm than this universe (a metaphysical order, idealist realities).

However it be symbolized and articulated, a moral dimension to human life has been perceived and affirmed. We have been aware not only of the profitable and the disadvantageous but also of the better and the worse, and have been inspired by some power to pursue the better; we have known that some actions are right, some wrong, and that it matters. At most times and most places, morality has been an integral part of the religious complex (although situations have on occasion arisen when the two have become historically dislocated—when a given form of religion has seemed not good; or to put it another way, when our sense of what is worthwhile, and the inherited symbols by which worth used to be formulated, have no longer converged).

If the panorama of our religious life is, in its outward form, selected mundane data symbolizing the more than mundane, then the task of students, or simply observers, of religion is to know those data but to consider them not in themselves but in their role in our lives. Their concern is not primarily the doctrines and scriptures and prayers and rites and institutions; but rather, what these do to a woman or a child. Not the tribal dance, so much as what happens to the African dancing; not the caste system, so much as what kind of person the Hindu becomes within it, or without it; not the events at Sinai, so much as what role the recounting of these events has played in both Jewish and Christian life over the centuries since; not the Qur'an so much as what the Qur'an means to a Muslim.

In illustration, let us consider as an example a statue of the Buddha, and take note specifically of one small part of it: the pose of the right hand. Among several such stylized poses used throughout the Buddhist world, we may choose just one, the *abhaya mudra* ('fearlessness pose'), in which the right arm is somewhat raised, that hand held straight up, palm facing out. Over and above the more universal significance of such a gesture (power, authority, benediction), in the Buddhist case this represents also an incident from the life of the Buddha, in which reputedly a wild elephant charging him and his group was stopped in its tracks when the Teacher raised his hand so, and became tame. The gesture gives artistic expression, then, to the Buddha's fearlessness in the face of the threat, and also to his conferring of fearlessness, and the grounds for fearlessness, on his disciples: his serene triumph over danger.

To say that this particular feature of sculpture symbolizes for Buddhists the overcoming of fear is to indicate not merely that it depicts an event in someone else's life, but also that it effects a change in one's own—since, to repeat, symbols not only represent but activate. The animal in its fury in the remembered anecdote may itself be taken as symbolic, representative of the pressures and assaults of life, which faith in the Buddha gives one the inner resources to withstand: the passions, for instance, to which such faith bestows on one the power quietly to say 'no'. To understand this particular item in the religious life of Buddhists, accordingly, is to know the history of how a Japanese emperor or a Thai merchant or a Chinese peasant through contemplating it in some nearby temple has had his life transformed, her fear removed, the personality healed. A parallel may be observed of the role in the lives of Christians, over the centuries, of the story of Christ's stilling of the tempest. His words, 'Peace, be still!' read in the Lesson, and the portrayal of the scene in stained-glass windows, have served to symbolize, for persons of faith, on the one hand Christ's power over the elements in his own life, and on the other hand the power that their faith in Him has in their lives, they have then found, to confer peace, to quell storms.

A special sort of symbolization, developed characteristically in, for instance, the Western world but by no means only there, has been the conceptual. A few recent philosophers have itched to legislate that concepts must be used to refer only to the sensible or phenomenal world; that it is illegitimate to use them symbolically to refer to a transcendent order. It would be manifestly stultifying to apply so austere a restriction to art or to most other human pursuits, apart from the natural sciences (from which these people have learned it). Such an orientation has seemed to work rather well with the 'objective' world—better, with the objective facets of the world (at least, until one raises moral questions about atomic bombs or ecology); but it appears stubbornly to misunderstand life in its distinctively human form.

One of the most powerful symbols in human history has, without question, been the *concept* 'God'. This concept, like other religious and other human symbols, has demonstrably meant different things to different persons and groups and ages; yet it is hardly too drastic an oversimplification to suggest that the concept has on the whole at least subsumed, integrated, deepened, and made operationally effective in the lives of many hundreds of millions of persons and in the life and social cohesion of many thousands of communities their awareness and their potential awareness of the entire range of transcendence with which they are surrounded or endued—of grandeur, order, meaning, aspiration, awe, hope, virtue, responsibility, rapport, integrity, worth, renewal. The highest, deepest, most comprehensive that they were capable of attaining, individually and socially, was organized, focused, and nurtured in and through this concept. (Given the distinction, observed by all believing theorists, between God and our ideas of God, such theorists may themselves make this same point by saying that God has used the idea of God to enter our lives; that the concept has served as a sacrament. More recent developments, with the concept 'God' no longer, for many, serving so effectively, as a symbol, will be touched on below.)

Although correlative conceptualizations are virtually worldwide and history-long, this particular concept was developed in its most powerful and characteristic form in the Near East and has permeated, at times dominated, the civilizations that have emerged from there to cover almost half the planet, especially the Islamic and the Judaeo-Christian. The Indian counterparts have been in many respects closely similar; in many, subtly different. China and Japan, although also employing symbolic concepts richly, have tended toward other religious and cultural patterns than this particular one.

Even so major a symbol, however, as the concept 'God', however all-embracing it may seem, is in the end significant not in isolation but within a whole system of ideas, practices, values, and the like, forming a pattern of which it is no doubt the keystone but not the totality. Certainly minor symbols like the pose of the right hand in a piece of sculpture or medium ones like the ceremonial holiness of the Sabbath, however significant they have been in the lives of many millions of persons, derive their meaning and their power from each being one item within a large pattern of symbolic structures, such as the Buddhist complex or the Christian.

And even these great complexes, each of which has an elaborate and ever-changing history, constitute systems to be understood not in themselves, as structures to be looked at, but rather in terms of the ambience that they make available for men, women and children to live within. 'In order to understand Buddhists, one must look not at something called Buddhism, but at the universe, so far as possible through Buddhist eyes.' It is not the symbols themselves that one must grasp, so much as the orientation that they induce: how the whole complex of symbols enables those who live in terms of it to see a sunset, a broken marriage, prosperity, the onset of cancer, one's election to public office.

The religious history of the Hindu community is a history, in part, of traditional ceremonial and ideological and sociological patterns. Yet in more significant part it is a history, however difficult this may be to discern, of fortitude and of quiet humaneness, of a conviction that life is worth living and death worth dying, that goals are worth striving for, that the immediate is caught up in the eternal. The Buddhist metaphors have served to kindle in the mind and heart of the Buddhist the perhaps unconscious awareness that one's own fortune is not a reason for gloating, or one's neighbour's fortune, for envy; that knowledge is more important than wealth, and wisdom than knowledge; that the world is to be appreciated and not merely exploited; that one's fellow is to be treated as an end, not merely as a means; that sorrow is not a reason for despair. Islamic law, theology, architecture, and the rest have been symbols that at their best have crystallized and nurtured, for Muslims, the courage and serenity, the sense of order and the aspiration to justice, the forbearance, the humility, the participation in community, that the Islamic system traditionally inspired. Christian symbols have given both form and actuality, among Christians, to many things, including for instance the ability of human suffering to become redemptive.

Of course, religious symbols and sets of symbols have been used also for mean and destructive purposes. Our wickedness, and not only our capacity for virtue, has been expressed and even encouraged by our symbol systems, at times. Through them we have found our freedom, our transcendence of the immediately given, our ability to move beyond being merely an organism reacting to its environment; but sometimes we have used these destructively, or have become victims of their inherent ambiguities. Nothing has turned a society into a community so effectively as religious faith: to share common symbols is about the most powerful of social cohesions. And yet few gulfs have been greater than those that separate differing religious communities, few hostilities so fierce as those between groups whose symbols differ.

Religious symbols do not raise us above the human level; only to it.

A final word about history. The history of religion has at times been mistaken for the history of its symbols; but this is superficial. The same symbols have discernibly changed their meanings over time, and indeed from person to person, and even within one person's life; also, persisting or widespread orientations and perceptions have been expressed in strikingly different symbolizations. The true history of religion is more deeply personalist—not in the sense of individualist: the personal is also the social, and especially so in the religious realm. The true history of religion, not yet written, is the history of the depth or shallowness, richness or poverty, genuineness or insincerity, splendid wisdom or inane folly, with which men, women, children and their societies have responded to such symbols as were around them. It is also, however, the tale, and to some degree this can be told, of when and in what fashion they have forged new symbols, or neglected or found themselves unable to respond to old. And nowadays especially it is also the story of how they deal or fail to deal with a plurality of symbolisms.

Our faith is in some sense the meaning that our religious symbols have for us; but more profoundly, it is the meaning that life has for us, and that the universe has, in the light of those symbols. For religious symbols do not 'have' meanings of their own; they crystallize in various ways the meaning of the world, of human life. There is a history of their varying ability to do this, at various times and places (or of our varying ability to have them do it).

How new symbols or patterns of symbols emerge is too complex or controversial a question to be summarized here; but how they develop once launched, how they are reinterpreted (sometimes radically) over the centuries, how their success in pointing beyond themselves often gives way to a rigidity and narrowness in which they or their institutions are prized or defended simply in themselves; how iconoclastic movements arise, to shatter the symbols (literally, smashing idols; or figuratively, attacking concepts and mores), whether in the name of something higher or out of misunderstanding, and often both; saddest of all, how a time may arrive when the symbols no longer serve a community, no longer communicate a transcendent vision, and then a profound malaise settles on the society and life comes to seem without meaning, and we become alienated from each other and even from ourselves and from the world in which we live. All this the historian can trace.

In recent Western history an aberrational tendency has arisen to imagine that human life is fundamentally or naturally 'secular', and that religion has been an added extra, tacked on here and there to the standardly human. This now appears to be false. Rather, the various religious systems have expressed varying ways of being human. The historian cannot but report that it has been characteristic of us to find that life has meaning and to formulate that meaning in symbolic ways, whether grotesque or sublime.

CHAPTER 2

History in Relation to both Science and Religion

Two great transformations characterize modern awareness, differentiating our age from all earlier eras. One, more conspicuous, derives from science, or from science-and-technology. The other, more subtle—and in the end, I shall suggest, more fundamental— is our awareness of history. Some contribution might come from reflecting at a first level on the relation between the two, that is, between scientific and historic awareness. Further, and more seriously, I will suggest that the relation between *religion* and science may in future be perhaps more truly and more manageably perceived in terms of the relation to each of modern historical consciousness. Between science and faith, historical awareness may mediate.

Science and faith both tend to appear absolute, when considered each in itself or each in relation to the other. Hence their collision. When considered each in relation to history, on the other hand, both are seen to be relative. At least, so I shall be arguing. God is perceived as beyond history, however active within it; and truth as transcendent to history, however immanent within it. Yet that is to anticipate. Whether or not my conclusions seem persuasive, in any case some may find illuminating and even perhaps cogent my preliminary theses, which will constitute their premises. What I am proposing is a vista within which our problem can be properly seen.

Both modern science, and modern historical awareness, are indeed modern, are novel. My word 'transformation' above is hardly an exaggeration; hardly even a metaphor. Admittedly, forerunners in each case can be traced far back to preceding ages. It so happens, moreover, that the Christian, and also the Muslim, communities have known early phases of both processes: those out of which present-day historiography and present-day science have grown. Indeed, both these communities have contributed to both. A comparativist is sensitive to these matters insofar as he or she contrasts, for instance, classical Hindu civilization on the issue of historical consciousness; or to a less degree, Far Eastern Buddhist on that of science. Nonetheless, twentieth-century science is radically different from anything that went before.

This is so, not only substantially, in its mightiness, range, finesse, precision, confidence, and much else. It is so also in the degree to which modern science permeates all our lives and suffuses our thinking, not only of course our acting, but our feeling and seeing and our aspiring and evaluating. Similarly, the modern apprehension of history is not only vastly more wide-ranging in its scope and deep in its knowledge; also it is quite new in the extent to which it, and the sense of unrelenting change that it signifies, dominate our perception of galaxies and languages and social institutions and concepts. All of these we now see as participant in process: as having always been changing and now changing before our very eyes.

Let us leave religion and faith aside for the moment; and consider simply the pair, science and history. Although both characterize modern consciousness, yet they have been largely separate, even disparate. Indeed, they have been in many ways contrasting. History is concerned with particulars, science with the general. History is chiefly concerned with the human, science with the nonhuman, objectively—and even in spirit science aims at being impersonal. History deals, among other things, with art and poetry and what men and women have deemed valuable, as well as with foibles and folly; science tries rigorously to exclude all aspects of the human that involve any reaching out beyond the immediately and empirically given. The two groups are educated in distinct parts of a university, take different degrees, and seldom collaborate. They have seemed to have rather little in common.

Despite this, on the other hand, there is the curious point that insofar as science has impinged directly, it might seem, on religion, in fact it has done so through the historical consciousness. It was when in the nineteenth-century West the Christian view of history was transformed for scientific reasons, with regard to geology and evolution, that an acute crisis arose; and Gibb, the most perceptive Western student of modern Islamic developments, has for instance remarked that it is primarily the historian with whom the Muslim modernist has to come to terms.

For some while, I have contended that a prime question for Western civilization will be to choose between two radically divergent options: whether to subordinate its views of human affairs—therefore, of human history—to its understanding of science; or *vice versa*, to subordinate its understanding of science to its sense of history and of the human. There are signs to-day, I believe, that it is at last beginning to choose the latter. For a good while, on the other hand, the opposite has been done.

It is not merely that some historians have tried to make historiography a science—at least a social science. This means that the natural sciences are seen as setting norms and goals and even methods and presuppositions. More important, humans were understood as modern science perceives them to be; and human history was deliberately reduced in thought to fit positivistic, naturalistic, scientistic dogmas. Furthermore, since modern science is thought of as being right, human history has tended accordingly to be perceived as having been in a sense wrong: pre-modern ages were interpreted as ignorant, superstitious, backward, and unfortunate. In the broadest possible terms, what was going on here was that the universe was perceived as natural science perceives it, and within *that* universe humans and human history were assigned their place—a subordinate and rather puny place, occupying a tiny span of time on a small planet wandering aimlessly around a minor star lost in a mediocre galaxy—and as, until modern times came along, thinking up odd ideas with little or no relation to truth.

The new view, just emerging, changes not the details of this, which in fact remain; but the framework and over-all structure. Rather than seeing ourselves as a minuscule item in the universe of science, we can rather look at science as one of the items in our historical attainment. Science is not a minor human achievement. Yet human it is: a human construct. It is one expression of one aspect of the human spirit. It has emerged historically; and like every other human activity it can best be understood historically, as in some sense subordinate to human development, and to time and place. It is one human achievement among others; with both the grandeur and the limitations that characterize our plenitude.

Like other great movements in human history before it, it began with enormous promise, worked itself out with brilliance, might, and spectacular success for a time. Yet its exceptional glory seems to have been matched by the fact that more quickly than any other comparable movement of the human spirit in the last ten thousand years, it has begun to show itself not only inadequate but unprecedentedly threatening, not only to the human spirit, but to our lives, our oceans, and our world.

Increasingly in the West, science is beginning to be confronted with a growing movement of disillusionment and of criticism, in the sense of adverse or negative evaluation. Its triumph is no longer undisputed. At the practical level there are those, especially among the youth, who reject—such as the hippies; or such as the bright young Ph.D. students in Physics who, to the bewilderment of their teachers, decide to abandon their studies in mid-stream because of distaste for the enterprise. At the theoretical level there are thinkers like Roszak who mount a brilliant and influential plea for alternative, more humane, outlooks. A few intellectuals have begun to criticize science and scientistic philosophy on strictly rational grounds, arguing that their logic is intellectually deficient.

All this is incipient only, however; and as yet, rather minor. A billion dollars annually continue to go into scientific research in even a small country like Canada: I quail to think what the figure may be in larger countries. Popular prestige continues high. Most telling, modern life in the West is so organized that to withdraw its scientific and technological underpinnings would mean that most people there would simply die forthwith.

My concern here, however, is not with a criticism of science, but with an understanding of it. This is still more recent, and still more narrowly based. Only a few spirits are as yet involved. Yet it will grow. By 'understanding' I mean historical understanding. Of the two great components of modern consciousness, science and history, it is my submission that in the final analysis the historical is inherently the stronger, intellectually. History can comprehend science, but science cannot comprehend history. When I say 'intellectually stronger', I realise that science may prove physically stronger. A fascist regime, or some counterpart to it, could incorporate science-and-technology and suppress historical awareness. That may happen. So long as the human intellect is free, however, the historian has access to more truth than does the scientist.

One significant landmark in this new development is the study by Thomas Kuhn, *The Structure of Scientific Revolutions*, first published in 1962 and in a slightly enlarged version in Japanese and English in 1969. This work is important, and may serve us here as symbolic, representative of the development generally, on two counts. The first has to do with what it says; the second, with the broad impact that it is having. It is, of course, a controversial book; and I myself do not agree with all its theses, particularly not with its theory of truth. Yet that is not the point. It has inaugurated, or anyway has illustrated, the deeply significant emergence of an historical understanding of science; a relativizing and making human of what claimed to be absolute. Of transforming consequence is the recognition that the achievement of science, the ideas of science, the so-called truths of science, are historically specific, historically limited, historically transient.

With this view, one does not debunk, one does not reject; one does not even criticize, in the negative sense of that word. Rather, one appreciates. One appreciates truly, accurately; by seeing both the ideas and the practical attainments of science as they in fact actually were and are—as particular ideas and particular practices at particular times and places: finite human constructs with no more claim to finality or to absoluteness than any other major human enterprise. In particular, Kuhn has done at the level of theory what ecology and Hiroshima have done at the level of practice: namely, to dissolve the eschatological pretentions of the scientific movement.

(The historian of religion reflects on the wryly humorous analogy between the emergence of historical criticism of the Bible and this new historical criticism applied to science a century later. The analogy may prove to be close.)

It is not the case, the historian here demonstrates, that science is moving in a straight line towards the truth; just as it is not the case that it is moving in a straight line towards the good. It has had some hold on truth, and it has had some hold on good, as have other movements of the human spirit in world history—the Buddhist, for instance, and the Islamic and the Christian. Yet that hold is finite, human, and historical. It is in process, in constant revision; and in constant need of revision.

One illustration which I myself have thought up—it is not from Kuhn—has to do with Copernicus, and his heliostatic theory. Sometimes his view is called heliocentric, but this is not quite accurate: in order to conform to his measurements, he located the sun at a short distance from the centre. Anyway, as everyone knows, for the view that the earth stands still while the sun revolves around it and, elaborately, the planets, he substituted the conception that the sun, rather, stands still, close to the centre of things, with the earth and planets circling about it. Indeed, on this innovating vision the modern scientific movement has by some been seen to be based. We now know, however, that in fact the sun does not stand still: it is much more vagrant than he ever thought the earth to be. And it is no nearer the centre of the physical universe than is our own planet. On these matters, we may see that he was wrong. Yet obviously he had a point!

Are we then to say that modern science is founded on an insight that is true, expressed in statements that are false?

To an historian of religion, that is entrancing. It is, however, too glib; and in my recent publications I have wrestled at length with the recognition, valuable both in science and in religion, that statements are in fact not in themselves either true or false, however great be the modern pressure to think so. The truth lies not in timeless propositions, but historically with persons and groups and the particular meaning that propositions have for them, and the insights that these convey. The historian sees science as he or she sees religion, not as true or false, absolutely; but as historical.

Thus we need not be critical of science; merely, realistic. Provided that we first participate in historical consciousness, we may then legitimately participate in scientific consciousness—without making fools of ourselves, and without losing our soul. In the particular phase of scientific development available to us, once we recognize it as that, as one tentative interpretation of one particular aspect of being human, we may intellectually participate with gratitude and loyalty, yet without idolatry.

Science does not deserve, and cannot have, our full allegiance; just because it is finite, human, and historical. Yet for those same reasons, we need not reject it, or condemn it. Rather, as we should of all human affairs, we should view science with both respect and compassion; and should share in it with a judicious mixture of admiration and reserve.

After all, it is *ours*. It is a sub-set of our human history. And the more deeply we appreciate its human and its historical character, the more truly shall we understand it; and the more precise will be our appreciation of it.

To say that it is finite, human, and in process—that it is historical—is to recognize that it is not The Truth. Yet this is not to say that its activities and ideas are at any given moment in no way true. The Truth is transcendent—is God. Yet transcendence is, God is, active in human affairs, is immanent in history; and humans, for all their finitude, for all their historicity, live in touch with God. In finite touch, in human touch, in historically particular touch, no doubt; and yet our lives are lived within the divine.

My first point, then, is that modern historical consciousness provides the framework within which scientific consciousness is to be embraced; to which subordinated: by which, interpreted. I am contending that this ordering is not only helpful, and not only rational, intellectually cogent. I suggest that it is also becoming inescapable: that intelligent persons who have not yet seen science so will presently come to do so. For the historical outlook is imperious, powerful, incontrovertible. Everything human, indeed everything that happens, happens within history. Except God himself, all truth is historical. And even God is involved in history, as well as transcendent to it.

My second point picks up the theological matter. For modern historical consciousness is large enough, and powerful enough, to comprehend not only science, but also religion; and what were once called 'the religions'. Some might agree with my first point but hesitate about this second; might hold, in traditional fashion, that other things and indeed other religions, are finite, human, and historical, but that their own religion—whether Islam or Christianity or whatever—is absolute, divine, and timelessly true. This is what scientists and scientistic philosophers have felt about the scientific enterprise: that it alone, unlike all other movements of the human spirit on earth, has the truth, or is firmly on its way to it, is in principle exempt from the limitations of finitude, humanness, and historical particularity. Alternatives are either wrong, or at best partial, they have held. Historians, and especially historians of religion, are quite familiar with this orientation. They observe it as arising at many times and places. Their task is not to debunk it, but to understand it—historically. And historically, it can always be understood. It seems quite evident, and readily demonstrable to the sensitive and informed, that what used to be called the religions are each finite, human, and historical—as well as infinite, divine, and timeless. This applies to one's own, as well as to others.

Each is a divine-human complex in motion. That is why careful historical scholarship separates each into two component elements: ones that I have called respectively 'cumulative tradition' and 'faith'. In faith, we are in touch with God. Or seen more largely, God—if we are to use that theist term—is in touch with particular men and women and children, at particular times and places, through particular mundane forms. Human history is and always has been in part mundane, transitory, finite; and in part, transcendent. For human beings, each in a particular earthly context, are in relation to God; faith is my name for that relation, wherever, and in whatever form, it occurs. More precisely it names the human side of the relation. The cumulative tradition, however, historical awareness is increasingly able to see, is finite, human, and historical. It is in constant process. To imagine that any is stable is now seen as an historically conditioned, historically understandable, error. Christian doctrines have evolved. They are still evolving. None is finally true. The Torah and the *shari'ah* (Jewish and Islamic 'Law') came into historical existence slowly; and to-day are in process of revision. And so on.

Neither science nor religion provides patterns that are firm; nor propositions that are true. God, however, is not a pattern; and God's truth is not a proposition. Scientific propositions, and Islamic or Hindu or Buddhist forms, mediate God's presence but are not themselves The Truth (as the mystics have long since known). Truth is personal, not propositional. These forms come and go.

As the Qur'an puts it, *Kulla shay'in fanin illa wajhuhu* ('Everything is evanescent, except His face').

It is a monumental fallacy of modern logic that propositions can be true or false. Propositions are also historical and mundane. What is true or false is what they mean to given historical persons. Through propositions, human beings may participate in truth; but the propositions themselves do not so participate.

The relation between science and religion is an historical rela-tion. Historical consciousness can understand it, and in some sense dominate it: can comprehend it, in both meanings of that term. By recognizing that science is finally subordinate to history, and that the cumulative religious tradition is so also, the historical con-sciousness can comprehend the issue between them.

In similar fashion, that consciousness, as comparative history of religion, can comprehend both Islamic and Christian move-ments, and the relation between *them*. The historian can see how both are true, and neither is. Unless one recognizes that both are true, and that both are false, one is a poor historian. We live in his-tory, and in history live with God. We to-day know that there is nothing beyond history except God. But nothing! Every single thing that human beings in the course of history have set up as beyond the historical, as semi-divine, is in process in our day of becoming revealed as not, after all, outside the grasp of the histor-ical process: of particularity, of relativity, of finitude. It has always been so; but only in our era are we becoming ineluctably aware of it.

Yet throughout history, we are also becoming aware, human beings have been characterized, less or more, by faith—sometimes in an Islamic form, sometimes in a Christian, sometimes a Hindu or a Shinto or a Tierra del Fuegan. And in faith, of whatever shape, less or more richly God has entered their lives. Religious patterns, ideas, forms, have not been eternal; yet the faith that these have generated, nurtured, and expressed, has been transcendently ori-ented. All else has been finite, human, and historical. In our next chapter, and again later in this collection, we shall be considering faith in philosophic and secularist forms: faith in reason, in truth, in science, and such.

Faith too has been these things and simultaneously divine. Faith is, has ever been, the historian can see, the point of intersec-tion of eternity and the human. Yet it is personal and its ever-changing forms are mundane.

Modern minds have been teased by the problem of science, technology, and the future of faith. Our consciousness can handle that problem with cheery confidence if we be historical, in the modern mode, and aware historically of science, technology, and the past of faith.

CHAPTER 3

Philosophia as One of the Religious Traditions of Humankind

The position to be propounded in this essay revives a thesis that has been set forth—or at least adumbrated—from time to time in the past by several highly reputable scholars, but has not been widely accepted, nor indeed in recent times been paid truly serious heed. I adduce a quite new range of evidence, from around the world; and suggest that the interpretation by being set in our new global perspective can in fact be seen as now solidly established— or at least can no longer be dismissed as casual or quaint but must be recognized as fully serious. Admittedly, the consequences of taking it seriously go deep, and ramify. One reason for its having been neglected when proposed in the past is doubtless that it unsettles fundamental presuppositions of modern Western cultural life; and indeed social and even political life as well. One speaks of 'pre'-suppositions advisedly, since to take the thesis seriously requests a reconsidering not of inherited convictions of our intellectual life only but too of certain of the categories within which those convictions have traditionally been formulated. Yet the modern awareness of history, long-range, comparative, planetary, our new vision of human life across the globe and across the millennia, has in recent times been developing so rapidly and so richly that it is in fact hardly surprising that it should now invite a substantial reinterpretation also of Western data, once one correlates with it also these. From the new vantage point of world history, an unprecedented self-critical self-consciousness is made available; and even, made requisite.

The thesis that we are about to consider is that the Greek tradition in Western civilization, rationalist-idealist-humanist (a tradition mediated then through Rome; so that it may equally be called the Graeco-Roman tradition, or the Western classical), is best understood when considered within the generic context of the various—other—religious traditions of humankind. It is neither absurd, nor trite, to re-interpret it as one of our planet's major religious (should one nowadays say rather, 'spiritual'?) traditions: different, of course, from each of the others (as these, of course, differed among themselves), yet comparable, and discerned most truly when so contrasted and compared.

In the comparative study of religion, the comparative history of religion (I always use a singular in those phrases), as in the comparative study of civilization, a corner is in process of being turned not unlike the corner that was turned last century in comparative anatomy, which eventuated in that case in the recognition of evolution: a new understanding of ourselves. The vision of evolution made discernible new relations among radically differing forms— without in any way distorting or glossing over the differences. Something of the sort is at issue here.

As remarked, a view that the Greek rationalist-idealist-humanist tradition is in some way 'religious' has been proposed sporadically, by classical scholars of the calibre of, for instance, Arthur Darby Nock, Festugière, and especially Jaeger.[1] To a considerable degree, this has signified in their minds, but even more clearly has been heard by those who read the proposals, as averring that there are significant similarities between it and the Christian and Jewish traditions (or, less clearly and less often, the religious patterns of the Greeks and Romans themselves), with which the West was familiar. Many might nod for a moment in passing agreement with a suggestion that there are similarities between, on the one hand, what I shall be calling philosophia, and, on the other, what they called religion. Yet they treated this as perhaps a curiosity, an interesting yet not engaging analogy, hardly more than a sprightly metaphor. Aware of more basic ways in which the two were for them drastically different, they were au fond unmoved.

Our present thesis is that these two are indeed profoundly different, and that yet they belong to the same species. Western civilization has two sources, one from Greece and Rome, one from Palestine. Its history is the development of these two, sometimes in harmony, sometimes in conflict, sometimes juxtaposed, yet never fused. It has developed the concept 'religion' to name (and even to reduce) one of them. It is important to understand, as can be done in the light of this duality, the proposition of the sociologist Werner

Cohn: 'that the West is the only culture in history that has a religion';[2] I would even say, the modern West. Yet the relation between these two is, in world perspective, a relatively minor instance of the question at issue. Let us turn to that world perspective; specifically, to the world history of religion.

It is not the case that 'all religions are the same'. Neither is it the case that they are so totally diverse as to render meaningless any considerations of them in relation to each other. The comparative historian of religion must report that every religious tradition on earth has been in some ways different from, and in some ways similar to, every other. Each is therefore to some degree unique; yet none but can be illuminated by being seen within the context of the others and of the whole. Any given tradition can be understood more truly when seen in the context of all.

Essentially, our argument will make three points. First, that our new awareness of humanity's religious history, and particularly our new understanding of traditions and systems strikingly different from any with which we had previously been familiar, as well as from each other, have induced a quite new appreciation of diversity: the sheer recognition that religious traditions differ profoundly among themselves not only in content but in form. We to-day see possible variations, and kinds of variation, both gross and subtle, of which previously we had not dreamed; the range of divergence of what is religious goes far beyond our earlier expectations, and indeed convictions. Secondly, the new insights, set in comparative perspective, have enabled us to recognize in a quite novel fashion the role of the religious in human life: the varying ways in which different persons, groups, classes, times interact with their religious institutions and ideas—with even the 'same' institutions and ideas. Thirdly, in the light of these new understandings we shall look specifically at the Greek legacy in Western civilization with more wide-opened eyes than in the past; and this will enable us, I shall argue, to see things that are obvious enough once noted but that previously we had no way of recognizing as variations on the larger theme.

More succinctly: first, we know better what a religious tradition looks like; secondly, we know better how a religious tradition works; thirdly, we can therefore understand better, more analogically, the Greek tradition in Western culture.

To put the argument in historical rather than logical form: I shall submit that the West's knowledge and understanding of religion (and of *homo religiosus*) began with the religious systems of the West, have recently been enlarged, and modified, to cover also those of the Orient, and are now ready to return to the West to comprehend also our Greek inheritance. So radically has our awareness changed as to be historically at a point where this reinterpretation of both religion and ourselves is now the next step.

Being an historian, I distrust precise definitions; since everything that I observe, I observe in process of changing. Rather than telling what religion is, we can describe and analyse what it has been, here and there throughout human history and across the planet. Further, one can argue that to know what it has been—never fully, yet with a knowledge always increasing—is not only more feasible but also more profitable, and more cogent, than a static definition. Nonetheless, it might be philosophically argued that within this historical approach lie covert theoretical positions, and that one cannot therefore quite hide behind that historical naiveté (or might one say, historical sophistication?). Nor am I insensitive to the classical query, how do I know what is to be studied as religious around the world unless I have already in my mind some notion of what is to be so characterized? How does the historian of religion select his or her data?

The answer to this will be illustrated by our present topic but has been illustrated to me dramatically also over the past forty years as I have excitedly learned all kinds of surprising new things in this realm, as I have explored the human scene historically. That answer is disarming: namely, that I do not know what is to be studied as religious until *after* I have studied. Admittedly I do have a hunch before I begin, which always turns out—delightfully—to have been partly wrong. No one can be a successful, or even a competent, historian of religion or comparativist who does not keep an open mind as to what kind of affair religion (or the religious) is. (There is also the point that to be competent in these realms requires that one's primary aspiration be to understand not religion so much as people—most of whom in most civilizations at most times have in fact lived in religious terms, as the West calls it.)

Personally, I have never found in practice any major problem here, even though I recognize that several of my friends are more aware of a difficulty in this realm and tend to feel that I am being evasive or obtuse. Accordingly, let us attempt to formulate in precise theoretical terms an assessment of this matter that may perhaps satisfy the rigorous theoretical analyst, at the same time as giving the historian both the freedom and the austere responsibility to go on exploring, however new the vistas to which the evidence may lead.

Here, then, is a proposed definition. It is based on the facts that the word and concept 'religion' comes linguistically and culturally from Western civilization, where at the end of the Enlightenment the concept was given a significantly new twist and in particular was used to conceptualize, and thereby to further, the growing bifurcation between what it designated and the rest of culture.[3] Latterly, there has been evolving a world-wide and a history-long reference. The concept itself is in process of historical development, and a definition accordingly must incorporate this dynamic. Accordingly, one may proffer this: the term 'religious' designates those matters in Western history that have generally been called religious there—specifically, Christian and Jewish tradition and faith—plus anything else on earth that is significantly similar. More operationally: . . . that can be shown to be similar.

The field of the comparativist historian is the study of differences and similarities between religious phenomena—not only between Christian and Hindu, but also between 15th-century Christian and 16th-century Christian, and between Bengali Hindu and Punjabi Hindu.

My proffered definition is conveniently vague. Do not seek precision, said Chuang tzu;[4] and I would say, seek precision in one's data, for religious history, but be suggestive rather than mechanical in one's insights. Our definition, in fact, is meticulously imprecise; rigorously open-ended. It starts with where we all are; or better, where we have come from, with an agreed and empirically observed base. And then it allows scholars to develop the concept as new knowledge and new insight are attained. Yet, it puts on them the burden of carrying the rest of us with them: the investigators must persuade their audience that what new thing they call religious, whether from Palaeolithic times or from modern Tokyo, deserves that name.

Most of us nowadays have, I think, little inkling of how recent has been in the West the discovery, with increasing breadth and increasing precision, of what have in fact been the various religious traditions of humankind. The story begins, of course, in its modern phase, with the Age of Discovery, with Western Christendom reaching out to the rest of the world, exploring, groping, probing, gradually becoming aware of peoples and places far beyond its previous horizon. There were brought back accounts, weird or wonderful, of other groups' religious doings—at first haphazardly, as travellers' tales, later in more ordered fashion and more abundantly. It was only the 19th century, however, that saw the rise of a serious attempt to give this matter systematic and disciplined consideration: actively searching out material, recording it carefully, scrutinizing it earnestly, interpreting it. This was the task of the universities, chiefly in Europe; it involved the learning of languages, the establishing and dating of texts, the ascertaining of rituals and social structures, the accumulation and the analysis of great quantities of data. The result was that the religious traditions of the world began to be known, in their historical array. It is difficult to realize with any vividness how great a change in Western consciousness all this has wrought. For we can hardly imagine now how ignorant we in the Western world recently were—for instance, at the beginning of the 19th century.

Some time ago I had occasion to examine the articles in this area in the successive *Encyclopaedia(s) Britannica(e)*: an illuminating and sobering task. Let us take the Buddhist example. In 1810 the fourth edition of the already mighty *Britannica* appeared in twenty large volumes. Like the earlier editions, it contains no articles on the Buddha or the Buddhist movement. This edition does, however, unlike it predecessors, refer in its article *China* to a 'sect of the idol Fo', as a pernicious superstition introduced from India contaminating the (deistic) 'purity' of the 'ancient religion of China'; and there is also a brief entry *Fo*, in five words: 'An idol of the Chinese'. Apparently one did not know, however, that *Fo* is the Chinese designation for the Buddha.

In the seventh edition, 1842, there is an article *Buddha*, 'one of the two appearances of Vishnu', who is said to have appeared thus in order to mislead the enemies of the gods, inducing them to take up false opinions and to reject the Hindu religion and hence to be destroyed. This is to be seen as reflecting a late Indian memory of a despised heresy. The eighth edition, 1853–61—and we are here into the second half of the 19th century—, in its article on *Japan* recognizes 'the religion of Buddha' as one of the religions of that country; and under the heading *China* there is at last mention of 'all the follies and absurdities of the doctrines of Buddha' as having been brought in and grafted on to the superstitions of the Chinese. It is, however, believe it or not, the ninth edition, 1875— that is, barely a century ago—in which one finds an article *Buddhism*.

Only recently, then, has the Western world been moving from a position of ignorance to one of information on the religious traditions of those groups with whom it shares this planet. (Curiously, Christian and Western-secular understanding both of post-Biblical Jewish and of Graeco-Roman religious life began to be serious only at about the same time.)

The 19th century closed, then, with an incipient awareness of the new data. Yet it will come as no surprise if one adds that those data were perceived still, at that time, in fundamentally Western patterns. The Western mind imposed preconceived forms on the information. At the turn of the century, it was standard in the West to think in terms of a series of entities, called 'the religions' of the world, to each of which a name was now assigned: 'Christianity', 'Hinduism', 'Muhammadanism', and the like.[5] Each was thought of as a formalized structure, more or less coherent, more or less stable, something that a person could 'have', but basically existing independently of the persons whose lives were informed by or constituted through it. Moreover, all tended to be thought of, in Western fashion, as entities among which one might choose: such that nobody should have more than one, and everybody could and theoretically did select which one he or she would have—or none. Further, the strong tendency at that time was to suppose that each was a system of belief, postulating that religious communities differed among themselves primarily by believing different things, and presuming that for each the question 'What do they believe?' was the central, and certainly a legitimate, question.[6]

We now know, for instance, that false perception of a religious position as a system primarily of belief arose partly because of the unusually prominent place of doctrine in the Christian system, and partly because of the one-sided Enlightenment background of European intellectuality at that time. By now we recognize that such a view distorts even the Christian case, despite the exceptional role of theology among Christians for many centuries as a central organizing principle and symbol. Scholars in due course learned that it certainly distorted other systems: that what is perhaps miscalled 'law', for instance, plays in the Jewish and the Islamic cases a role comparable to that played by theology in the Christian, organizing and giving coherent structure to the various parts of the complex, so that in those instances the counterpart, for instance, to orthodox and heretical is, rather, orthoprax and deviationist. It came to be recognized also that often in Africa, for instance, a tribal dance, and not a set of doctrines (nor of laws), might be the central pattern.

Furthermore, it became recognized also that in some instances the religious complexes of various groups were not organized by any central principle into systematic cohesion: that some evinced a congeries of not necessarily coherent symbols, and indeed some delighted in such exuberance. The notion that 'a religion' should be a form, coherent, structured, stable, systematic, proved to be characteristic of certain types, among many others.

Historically also, particularist expectations gradually dissolved in widening knowledge. Western thinkers—not least, of course, Protestants—have operated with what I have ventured to call the 'big-bang' theory of religious history. I have developed this notion at some length in a recent publication;[7] here let me say simply that by it I refer to the idea that a religion begins with one great seismic event, as it were: a striking happening within history, in the reverberations and resonances of whose explosive power down the succeeding ages subsequent generations of the faithful live. According to this view, the true form of a religion is its original form, which is ideally stable. I call this a Protestant view: aphoristically, for Roman Catholics Christian truth is what the Church teaches, for Anglicans what it has taught, for Protestants what it taught originally, in the *kerygma*. Yet all types of Christian have tended, especially recently, to think of the final truth of Christianity as located fundamentally in the first century A.D.

To this was added a further notion, one that saw each religion as a kind of additive to history, and to human nature—postulating ourselves as basically secular, with a religion as something over and above, which some people for this or that reason choose to have. Thus the religion comes to be thought of as something that has been injected (or is alleged by believers to have been injected) into the temporal or secular or real world from the outside and that remains there as a more or less established extra, available to men and women in more or less purity depending on how close to its pristine form they are able to get hold of it.

Now I would argue that this sort of understanding is false even in the Christian case; is religiously distorting. I have contended, on both theological and historical grounds, that it is not the case that the first is the most important Christian century. The Islamic process has been a constantly on-going movement, religiously new every morning. The Buddhist movement is not to be understood solely or even primarily in terms of the teaching, or even the personality, of the Buddha.

Moreover, and however that may be, the comparativist discovers further that even such so-called 'founded' religions of the world are at best one type among others. This is so, even if comparativist study does not lead one, as it has led me, to feel that the big-bang interpretation is a misconception even in those instances: that continuous creation, whether theological or humanistic, is a much more apt metaphor. In any case, it turns out that there are many religious complexes that do not have any particular beginning point in time, and would not be interested even if they did. (The Hindu instance is salient, though not alone.) For these, the truth does not lie in the past, nor come from the past, but in the present, or a timeless realm accessible always in the present; and that truth is not, never was, in a systematic form, or a conceptualizable pattern. It may, rather, take the form of an experience, or a process, or a personal quality, or a communal participation. Indeed, the notion of 'truth', with or without a capital T, may or may not be applicable. (Nor, one may add, the derived notion of falsity. The idea that a religion may be untrue, especially in the sense that its beliefs are such, is a peculiar modern-Western emergence.)

Here too a development in our understanding can be historically illustrated. In the *Oxford English Dictionary*, about 1891, the entry 'Buddhism' reads: 'Buddhism. The religious system founded by Buddha'. The 1971 *Webster New Collegiate Dictionary's* entry reads rather: 'Buddhism. A religion of eastern and central Asia growing out of the teaching of Gautama Buddha that . . .'. One may notice that while the earlier presentation focuses on the past, speaks of system, and of founder, and is tacitly oriented to India (the point of origin), the more recent begins with the present-day, with the further Orient, speaks in terms of growth, and is generally much closer to being amorphous, although it still uses the -*ism* form and the phrase 'a religion'. (It also uses 'teaching' in the singular and allows itself to summarize that teaching in a mere eighteen words which follow.) Given our present scholarly awareness, presumably twenty-five years from now dictionaries will be speaking rather in terms of a complex of movements, across the centuries and across many areas. We now see that most religious persons throughout history have been not carriers of a pattern, but participants in a process.

The religious traditions, then, differ among themselves radically, both in structural form and in historical form. Not only so, however; also, again radically, and again not only at the actual but at the theoretical or ideal level, they differ in the relation to themselves of what Westerners used to call their members or adherents. The formalized pattern of the Church was responsible for the impression that a religion is something that has members, and boundaries, and is optional. The Christian Church is a designatable and organized institution, to which a person formally does or does not belong, one that he or she may enter or leave—in theory at their own option (they may also be forced out, or even forced in). No one is born a member of the Church (as one is born a Jew; though a child may become a Christian through baptism when but a few days old). The Islamic, though its form is certainly not the same, is in various ways comparable; the Jewish, less so. In these two cases the differences are major, as well as the similarities. In the Muslim world there is, for instance, nothing corresponding to the Church. Once one gets to know a wider range of instances of religious complexes, however, it turns out that they vary over a wide gamut, even among those that moved away from the situation where, as in the Andaman Islands, the boundaries of the religious pattern are co-terminous with those of the socio-cultural group.

At one end of this gamut are closely-knit structures that permit no conversions either in or out. No outsider may become a Druze, or (at least until World War II) a Parsi; and no one within those groups may, theoretically, leave them. At the other end are complexes that have no organization at all, and no definition; and certainly nothing that could be called a membership. Some Western scholars have tried to estimate how many Taoists there are in China. This is not quite so misconceived, perhaps, as asking how many pragmatists there are in America; but almost. The estimated number of Buddhists plus that of Shintoists in Japan far exceeds the population total.

Earlier this century, books were written in the West with titles such as *The Three Religions of China*;[8] I still remember how bewildered undergraduates were thirty-some years ago—a much less sophisticated generation than the current group in these matters—by such uncouth textbook phrases as that in China a person could 'belong to three religions at the same time'. I had my work cut out attempting to elucidate to them, and to criticize for them, those inept formulations. 'Three religions' was, of course, a mistranslation of the phrase *san chiao* ('three traditions'), itself a concept with an intricate and subtle history. Actually, if one were going to move in this direction, a Westerner might well speak rather of four religions in China. For popular animism, with no organization, no membership, no conscious recognition, yet surely numbered many times as many 'practitioners' as any of the classical three (if one be resolute to think of numbering). It is instructive to reflect on the different sorts of history that its counterpart has had in Japan. This is partly because in the Japanese case the primitive indigenous religious complex was, by observers thinking in Chinese, given a name ('Shinto', which some centuries later also got translated into Japanese). It is interesting to note what conceptualization can do to a movement.

To mention another instance of divergence: of the five great missionary movements in world history, the first three were religious. (I reckon the fourth and fifth to be the Marxist, and the Western secular.) The first of these, the Buddhist, differed from the next two, the Christian and then the Islamic, in that the Buddhist missionaries, in all their compassionate zeal, as they moved across most of Asia, did not ask or expect that those who listened and responded to their message should abandon what other religious involvements they might already have. (Christian baptism formally involved a rejection of alternatives.) The result has been that from Ceylon to Japan those whom Westerners call 'Buddhists' are in almost every case also and simultaneously participants in at least one other religious complex—what is sometimes called *bön* in Tibet; what has been called '*nat* worship' in Burma; Taoist or what Westerners call 'Confucian' in China, or both; one of these or 'Shintoist' or both or all three, in Japan.

Over against these missionary enterprises, which themselves differ, let us turn to a highly sophisticated but usually non-missionary religious outlook, that traditionally of the Hindus. In modern times some Westerners, with their own presuppositions about the form and function of a religious system, becoming familiar with and then impressed by Hindu orientations, think of themselves as 'converted' and decide 'to become a Hindu'. The first person in history who ever became a Hindu from the outside seems to have been an aggressive European lady in the late 19th century.[9] There have been various Westerners in this century who would follow. This indicates that they have missed the point of what they are considering. Any outsider who wishes to become a Hindu has misunderstood a fundamental Hindu outlook. A sophisticated Hindu might well say: 'What: adopt *these* means? These symbols? Haven't you some of your own? The people in the next village have different ones. And it remains at the level of superficial outward form, to shift from one set of symbols to another. The point is to see that dimension of reality of which the forms are only a reminder, and to which they are a response. The point is to see the richness of the world in which we (and you) already live. To change one's religion is to move horizontally; not vertically—side to side, whereas the whole point is to reach up, and to dig down.'

To change one's religion is, from such a perspective, like someone who is taking pictures with black-and-white film, and meets someone else who has colour film, and colour pictures—and says: 'Oh, I must take a picture of *your* temple; it looks so much richer than mine.' And of course the point is, the kind of film that one is using; not where one points the camera. As Gandhi put it: 'I would no more think of asking anyone to change his religion than I would think of changing my own.' This diverges substantially from traditional Western postulates, and especially the 'either/or' mood, and the almost fierce conviction that one can be a 'member' of one, and of no more than one, system at a time. I sometimes tell my students that it is only my being Hindu that enables me to be both Christian and Muslim at the same time.

One need not go on. Essentially, all that I am saying is that our enlarged awareness has meant a shifting from an earlier notion that the so-called religions of the world were structures of differing content but similar form; shifting to a recognition—even should one not go so far as I do in saying that there are no religions, no fixed systems, no entities—at least that various traditions are often cast in radically differing form. And so far as content is concerned, one begins to realize that a quite new type of query is required. There has been a progression from imagining that the various traditions gave differing answers to fundamentally the same sorts of question, through a phase of recognizing that they were asking differing questions, and more recently to a discovery that some were not asking or answering questions at all.

I have over-elaborately made a very simple point: that it turns out that the religious traditions of the world do not look alike. The more carefully a comparative religionist studies the world scene, the greater the variety that he or she discovers; the more striking the differences among religious traditions. In a sense, to the old question as to what do the religious systems of the world have in common, it would hardly be an exaggeration now to give a rather simple answer: namely, 'nothing'. At least, nothing of central significance to each. Or at least, this is nearly true, objectively. The religious traditions of the world do not look alike. And the more closely one studies them, the more divergent they are seen to be.

This brings us back to the definitional point. If they have nothing in common, why do we call them all 'religious'? The answer to that is again fairly simple: namely, that their religiousness lies not in themselves, but in the orientation that persons have to them. I said just now that they do not resemble each other objectively. But neither are they religious objectively.

Perhaps I over-state my point. Let me rather put it this way: that there is no way of telling that a tradition is a religious tradition by looking at it. What makes it religious is the way human lives are affected by it.

The various religious traditions of the world—and this statement holds even if one thinks only of the major traditions: the Christian, the Jewish, the Islamic, the Hindu, the Buddhist, the

Chinese—are not the same, in institutional pattern or in social role. They are not the same in orientation or in historical development. They are not the same either in content or in form.

Why then do we call them all 'religious'? An inadequate reply might be, because they are to some degree similar in function. It is the role that they have played in human life that makes them, along with their differences, comparable. The locus of the religious, as I have been increasingly finding and asserting for some decades, is persons, not things. There are no inherently religious data; they become religious in relation to personal life.

(Before we proceed, one must perhaps make this observation: we have moved beyond that recent phase in Western cultural history, I trust, when individualism was so dominant that by 'personal' one would suppose that 'individual' is meant. There is no polarity between the social and the personal. The opposite of 'individual' is 'social'; the opposite of 'personal' is 'impersonal'. One may note that a society may be personal or impersonal. And one may aver that an individual can become a person only in community. To be a person is to be involved in the polarity between the social and the individual.)

The locus of the religious is the personal, in human interaction with one or another of the diverse and complex traditions of humankind. If I may reiterate a theme song of mine: 'to understand the religious life of Buddhists, one must look not at something called "Buddhism", but at the world—so far as possible, through Buddhist eyes'. The significance of Buddhist data for us is their meaning for Buddhists. What makes the material of the Buddhist tradition religious for Buddhists, and significant for us, is the fact that because of their relation to some of that material, certain Buddhists are enabled or inspired to deal in a certain way with the world around them: with the crying of a neighbour's child, the beauty of a moonlit lake, the meanness of a local moneylender, the joy of a village festival, the onset of inoperable cancer.

The religiousness of religious symbols and of the tradition that they constitute does not lie in those symbols or that tradition. These, it turns out, may be of stunningly diverse sorts, of no constant shape or style. It lies rather in the involvement with or through those symbols of those persons or groups whose lives are ordered in relation to them. That involvement leads far beyond the symbols themselves, demanding or making possible the totality of the person's or the group's response, and affecting their relation not only to those symbols but to themselves, to their fellows, and to the stars.

To this involvement I give the name 'faith'. This is at one level that quality whereby persons become religiously involved in or through the data of their tradition. It is, from another angle, the meaning that the tradition has for them, if they are involved; and further, the meaning that life and the universe have for them, in the light of their involvement.

It is their faith that makes the tradition religious, at least as much as *vice versa*. If I sing a hymn or observe a liturgy or repeat a creed mechanically, nothing happens; but if I do it as an expression of faith, however weak, it becomes in turn an evocator of faith both for me, since my own faith is thereby enlarged, and for my neighbour or for my children. The forms of any tradition function as occasions for faith not in themselves, but insofar as persons are actively involved with them. The temples of ancient Egypt once served to inspire and to crystallize the faith of persons; now they are but tourist attractions. The ideas of the Manichees once served as channels of faith for millions; now they are but the subject of Ph.D. dissertations in history.

One may say, of course, that this propounds a somewhat new meaning for the old word 'faith', a meaning that has as yet not become widely established. This is only partly true, and in any case I believe that the situation will change; indeed is already in process of changing. The matter here is much the same as recently with the notion 'religion': there, as we have seen, Westerners began with a concept that fitted at first only those instances of the religious with which they had become familiar in the West, and presumed at first that other instances, though different in content, would be similar in form; but as knowledge grew realized that they had seriously to modify and to refine, indeed to refashion, the concept. The conception of 'faith' has not yet gone through the comparable process, and most people do not yet have available to them a notion of faith that will serve to accommodate not only Christian faith but Islamic, Buddhist, Hindu, ancient Sumerian, Bantu, and the others. (More generally: most people do not yet have available a notion of faith that will accommodate not only their own faith but other peoples'.)

Some Christian theologians, especially in Germany, have even explicitly resisted this transformation, affirming that other people have religions while only Christians have faith. Some secularist thinkers also have resisted it. Being hostile or indifferent to Christian faith, or Jewish, they have been insensitive to faith generally, or have denied it altogether as a fundamental, let alone a universal, human category. Such resistance is waning, however; and in any case, is untenable. What is required is the positive attainment of an adequate perception, with the construction then of a viable conceptualization. As I have said, some of us are working at this. Indeed, it is in the process of attempting to understand faith simultaneously in its Christian and its oriental religious instances that one comes to realize that the refashioned understanding of it in world perspective makes one potentially aware also of its occurrence in our own culture in previously unidentified forms.

A 'religious' tradition, then, is one that has expressed, elicited, nurtured, and shaped personal faith. A tradition is religious if, or insofar as, it has done this. And should one ask what 'faith' is, the answer may be called either circular or historical, at will (yet with our earlier definition of 'religious', it makes coherent sense): that faith is that human quality that has been expressed in, elicited, nurtured, and shaped by, humanity's religious traditions. It is ineffable. Yet that is all right; so too are most other significant human qualities—love, courage, hope, joy, alienation, despair. We must hammer out new conceptualizations that will help us as intellectuals to discern and to understand it. Let us not imagine, however, that we can 'define' faith, in the sense of capturing it within a formula. Any conceptualization in order to be helpful must be squarely based on the historical data that we have affirmed. Faith, I repeat, and this is its only possible non-transcendentalist 'definition', is that human quality that in diverse forms has been expressed in, elicited, nurtured, shaped by, our human religious tradition. (The transcendentalist definition that I would proffer, for those willing to think in such terms, is: faith is the human relation to, involvement in, positive response to, the Transcendent.)

I have now articulated—sorely inadequately, I realize—my two major points: that in comparativist perspective traditions look different, each from the others, and second, that they are comparable in that they have served some sector of humankind symbolically as that in relation to which they could live a life of faith. We turn now to my final question: whether these considerations contribute anything to a possible interpretation of what I am calling *philosophia*.

One will not fail to have noticed that when I assert that one cannot tell that a given tradition is religious just by looking at it, the implication, important for our purposes, is that one cannot tell that a given tradition is *not* religious just by looking at it. That it does not look like what we have previously thought a religious tradition to be, is neither here nor there.

I use the word *philosophia* rather than its modern derivative 'philosophy' in order to suggest that what is under consideration here is that animating and commanding love of wisdom of which, historically, specific philosophic systems or patterns of ideas have been the crystallized expression, as it were: the intellectual deposit; and I specifically wish to include also the idealist and humanist and rationalist dimension of the Greek tradition. In fact, if I had to use an English term rather than the Greek original, for what I have in mind, it would be not 'philosophy' but the Latin-derived 'rationality'; perhaps, humanistic rationality.

Obviously I contend that our question is not whether this tradition looks like what we know of the world's religious traditions, which to many it does not—just as no one of them looks like the others. It is a question, rather, of what it has meant to persons who have lived their lives in terms of it. I have written above that the concern of the student of religion is not the tribal dance, so much as what happens to the African dancing. Not the caste system, so much, as what kind of person the Hindu becomes within it, or without it. Not the *mudrā* of the statuary, so much, as how a Buddhist is changed by contemplating it. Not the Qur'an, so much as what the Qur'an has meant, in differing ages, to the Muslim.[10]

It seems fair, then, to apply the same assessment in this realm. I am concerned not specifically with what Plato or Aristotle said, nor with the plays of Sophocles, nor the art of Praxiteles; but with the movement of the human spirit that over the centuries in Western life since, these things inspired, nurtured, and were felt to express. This tradition has been conspicuously different objectively from the Christian and the Jewish. That is clear. Yet it has been no more different from these, I am suggesting, than they in their turn have been from the Hindu; nor than the Shinto has been from the Islamic, or from the Buddhist; and at the same time no less similar, so far as personal involvement goes, than all these have been among themselves.

In Western cultural history, I am suggesting, humanism, idealism, metaphysics, and the idea of rationality, as over the centuries they have been articulated and re-articulated in our life in the legacy that stems from Greece, have provided persons and society with a complex of patterns in terms of which they have been able to organize their lives, and to find them meaningful; to find coherence in the universe, to attain coherence within themselves, and to coordinate these two; to dedicate themselves to goals discerned as worth striving for, with courage and loyalty and discipline strong enough to overcome both external and internal pressures of lesser worth. This, a comparativist well knows, is the stuff of faith.

Humanism, for example: not as a specific doctrine but as a vision, a faith, related to the Greek legacy and haunting Western life, with a sense of the human as the final mystery and final worth, final truth. There is no question but that this was immensely strengthened in the West by the Christian doctrine of incarnation: God in human form. *Vice versa*, however, also: one may argue that Greek humanism has strengthened the West in its apprehension and probably even its formulation of that Christian doctrine. I have long been interested in the point that, of the three major sectors of the Christian Church in the middle of the first millennium A.D., the Latin-speaking, the Greek-, and the Syriac-, at that time roughly co-ordinate, the last almost *en bloc* presently chose to become unitarian Muslim, while the other two remained trinitarian Christian; so that one is tempted to speculate whether the Semitic-speaking group perhaps never did quite understand Christian doctrine in its Greek metaphysical forms, in general, and theories of the incarnation in particular. Islamic studies in general, and the history of Greek philosophy in the Arabic world, are both subtly illuminating for one's understanding of humanism.

Secondly, idealism. 'The idea of perfection in the Western world',[11] is a resonant and suggestive phrase. The history of ideals in Western thought and life and feeling; the orientation to beauty, justice, truth, and the like; the dynamic power with which these concepts have lent themselves to people's ordering of their lives into significance and growth: obviously these have been momentous matters.

Are we suggesting that other people have had no ideals? If one considers ancient Israel, and the Bible generally, may one not say, aphoristically, that they did not have ideals, they had God. It would be an over-simplification, no doubt, yet hardly a distortion, to say that the persons portrayed in and inspired by those sources did not pursue justice (explicitly), but obeyed the Most High. Do these not come to the same thing? Yes, of course—but via differing routes: that is precisely our point.

Even humanism has regularly been a metaphysical ideal. The famous asseveration, 'man is the measure of all things', has from the beginning had two divergent theoretical interpretations. In one it has enunciated a theory of individualist relativism, which critics have seen as not viable, both socially and intellectually chaotic. In the other interpretation, it has postulated a humanism, which on occasion has been as transcendence-oriented as Christian theology or Hindu speculation. In this latter sense as a humanist motto it has widely been taken as referring to 'man' as a metaphysical ideal, and to actual empirical men, women and children insofar as and because empirical human beings participate, by being human, in the metaphysical, cosmic, prototype. Such a position was carefully developed by various early thinkers and has been implicitly or explicitly consequential down through the centuries since. It was explicitly rejected by others; and that tradition too has had a following since: understanding the human in an empirical but not a metaphysical sense.[12]

It is probably fair to say that the latter view has been considerably less influential in most of Western history until very recent times. In any case, and in line with our general theme, there is still a question as to whether even the minority who have adopted the non-transcendentalist interpretation in theory, have in practice lived lives outside what the others interpret as a transcendentalist humanism.

For that humanism, in Western society, the standard for measurement of all things has been actual persons no doubt but only derivatively, and primarily Cosmic Man or Woman,[13] the ideal to which actual human beings do or may approximate. Of course, this has enormous consequences for one's dealing with actual human beings, both oneself and one's neighbour; indeed, for one's attitude both to past history and to the future. There are remnants of the force of this metaphysical (that is, transcendent) intellectualization—or we may say, symbolization—in modern talk, and feeling, even among persons who are certainly not aware of how involved they are in a transcendent metaphysics: when they say that Hitler's treatment of Jews was inhuman; or speak of a dehumanizing effect of technology, or of modern society as impersonal; or say that minorities have certain rights.

I am one of those who hold that no one has reasonable grounds—has any 'right'—to talk about human rights who rejects metaphysics. I personally, that is, side with the interpretation of humanism in the cosmic sense; and feel rather strongly that the other conceptualization of it involves both logically and historically a tendency to undermine the very values that it theoretically posits—adducing recent Western developments as supporting evidence for my view. Yet insofar as those of us who hold this idealist view may conceivably be wrong, insofar as the other side be right in contending that it is both reasonable and, over a span of generations, practical to pursue the humane virtues without transcendent ground, to that extent the divergence does not matter. If they be right, then the humanist tradition in both its wings, not only the until recently predominant and loftier one, has been for the West theoretically as well as in practice a religious tradition.

Thirdly, and most centrally: reason. This particular point repays a little developing. We come back to the matter of symbols. Faith has to do with transcendence: the ability to live in terms of, in relation to, the more than mundane. Religious symbols have to do with the fact that we humans point to that which we cannot see, feel about that which we cannot touch, speak and think about that which goes not only beyond the empirical but beyond the reach of our words and our minds; and we do these things by the use of symbols. As we have seen above, a religious symbol is some item from within the immediate world that symbolizes for some persons what transcends the immediate world. A fetish, an 'idol', a scripture, have played this role, as a locus and focus of transcendence: the point where the eternal is seen as breaking through into time, where a more or less concrete bridge is constructed or made available between the infinite and the finite.

At the most sophisticated levels, more subtle matters have been involved. In the Jewish and the Islamic instances, for example, it is to some extent morality that is thus consecrated, is discerned as holy, so that righteousness is where the divine and the human meet; righteousness becomes the mediator between God and the human person. Insofar as one acts justly, one participates in transcendent reality. Everything else in our lives we share with the natural world; but justice we share with God. (My vocabulary here is Greek.) And to live in accord with the moral law is to order one's life into coherence, loyalty, meaning. In the Christian case, it is the person of Christ that primarily serves as this mediator, this symbol. (In this and in other cases, of course, there is also the concept 'God': lately I have been developing the idea that the concept of God has served as a sacrament over a wide sector of human history; in theological terms, God has used the idea of God to enter human lives.)

Now in the Greek case, and in the philosophic tradition stemming from Greece, this rôle has been played by reason. Reason, which the outsider, the non-metaphysician, regards as a human, evolutionary construct, the Greeks among us regard as a transcendent order, in which human beings participate—fumblingly, falteringly, but salvifically. Empirical human reasoning is seen as an approximation to Reason with a capital R. One might speak of Natural Reason, to contrast with positive reason, by analogy with Natural Law in contrast to positive law.

In this vision, intellect and truth are seen and felt not as instruments, by means of which we pursue our goals and implement our purposes, therefore as finally subordinate to us; but rather as higher than we, to which we subordinate ourselves, by which we discover what goals are worth pursuing, what purposes we shall serve, and even what we ourselves finally are. Also, it is the principle by which we discover what the world around us is; it is that which relates us to the universe. The oft-cited phrase 'a human is a rational animal' (*anthrōpos zōon logikon*)[14] might be rendered, a human is essentially a living being who participates in the ultimate order of the cosmos. This too was explicitly recognized and developed by the Stoics, and in the Stoic-Platonic-Aristotelian synthesis after the first century A.D. Such an interpretation was explicitly rejected by the Epicureans and by the Sceptics. I am suggesting, however, that it is in its more transcendent connotation that it too has been chiefly effective in the Western world over most of the last two thousand years. I would feel, although some would disagree, that this has in fact been the case even for those who did not recognize it explicitly, at the theoretical level. (One might even remark that for the Greeks the saying avers that rationality has become incarnate in the human.)

Reason here is seen as the ultimate principle of the universe; also as the central and crowning principle of the human. Reason is the mediator between what others might call the human and the divine; we participate in the divine insofar as our ideas are true— and more actively, our behaviour rational.

This means not only that one may legitimately, and perhaps even imperatively, spell Truth with a capital T. It also means that the intellect serves as our integrating principle. This is so both socially (rationality is the link among persons in society, and the principle of social order), and individually (to behave rationally is moral). Thus through this symbolization three things are accomplished: the universe around us is seen as endowed with coherence and order; our personal life becomes endued with coherence and order; and the two are linked, indeed integrated.

This is faith.

Faith in one of its forms, at least.

Intellectuals, accordingly, have ideally been those whose commitment and loyalty to, faith in, intellectual pursuit have been total: not only passively, in that they would follow wherever the evidence or the argument might lead, but actively, dynamically, so that they would strive, restlessly, to search out new evidence, to think through new arguments, rejecting all that is not intellectually convincing, and striving to understand the world. Such persons at their best are monotheist: for them, truth, justice, beauty, and love—including, if they are also Christians, the redemptive love of a man on a cross—are ultimately one; these do not constitute a congeries of disconnected values. Also, human integrity itself is finally one also with these other virtues, which appear separate only from a distance. Such persons are not henotheist: not the kind of intellectual who worships truth alone among the several virtues, and thinks of the intellect as one aspect only of life, coordinate somehow with (or disparate from) various others. Rather, for the true intellectual the intellect is that by which the personality is unified, the parts are made coherent. Nor are they polytheist, pursuing truth during the week, but God on Sunday; or pursuing the intellect and its tasks from 9 to 5, but pursuing love and community at home, and joy on the week-ends.

Ideally, such an intellectual is a dedicated, integrated, activated, courageous, serene person of faith, freed from the distractions of personal whims and material enticements. In actuality such a person may approximate this ideal only distantly; but it is the ideal that informs and controls—or may we not say, liberates—his or her life. The approximation in any actual case is probably as distant or as near, roughly, as has been the case for other types of faith, either in the West or in the rest of the world.

Such, then, is our thesis: that the Greek legacy in the Western world is to be seen as similar to, as well as different from, those half-dozen or so major religious traditions in human history through which human life, both individual and social, has in various ways been structured.

One difficulty, one might feel, is that my contention is overly persuasive; to the point of being jejune. Does it prove too much, becoming unfalsifiable? For my point is not demolished by a pointing out of differences between our Greek heritage and the world's admittedly religious traditions. Them of course I recognize and cheerfully admit; for there has been no religious tradition on earth that has not evinced stark and significant differences from all the others. When comparative religion was getting under way, there used to be discussion as to whether Christianity is not unique. The comparativist at first was thought of as disputing this; and the issue was emphasized. By now, rather, that comparativist has discovered that 'of course'; every religious system is unique.

Nor is our thesis to be gainsaid by affirming that the differences are crucially more significant than the similarities. Every conservative Christian affirms that what is distinctive in Christian faith and the Christian tradition quite outbalances any similarities that the comparativist may ferret out to other systems; and the same goes for the conservative Muslim, or Buddhist. And they may well have a point. It is not the business of comparativists to tell the Christian, or the Muslim, or the Buddhist—nor indeed the Western rationalist—that in stressing the distinctive they are wrong. The task is not to prove anything, but to understand.

The comparative religionist, as I held at the beginning, is not urging that similarities are more significant than differences; only that they are illuminating. Both are illuminating. The case rests on the contention that, however unique a tradition may be, it can nonetheless be more accurately, more penetratingly, understood if seen not in isolation, but in relation to the others and to the whole. Similarly here: the thesis is not that the Greek tradition in the West is no better than the great religious traditions of our globe, nor no worse than they, nor no different from them.

At least, one may surely press an appeal to rationalists in the West to become self-conscious about the relativism of their stand. Yet one may also be prepared to find them resisting this, as Christian thinkers similarly for long resisted having 'Christianity' see itself, and theologically interpret itself, as 'one religion among others'.

As we have remarked, we are not the first, by any means, to suggest that the tradition may best be seen as religious; or, as comparable to 'a religion'. Yet my impression is that in such cases the judgement has tended to be thought of, or at least to be heard, as a metaphor. The present thesis is in line with those suggestions, but goes beyond them in, perhaps, two ways. The first is our historical understanding: we are speaking of not the Greek vision in itself, nor in its early phases, but in the continuing legacy that has developed from it consequentially in the life of the Western world down over the centuries. Secondly, we are contending that, in the light of the comparative history of religion now available to us, the matter is no metaphor, but must be taken seriously as straightforward description. There are still many persons, not least in our universities—whether they think of themselves as anti-religious or not—who hold that 'religion has no place in the university', unaware that this is a self-contradiction. (Nor perhaps is the development in the United States that has transformed the separation between Church and State into a dichotomy of religion and politics, coherent or viable: insofar as religious conviction nurtures honesty, is honesty in politics to be ruled unconstitutional?)

Where, then, have we arrived? Let me close by enumerating swiftly a few items that may perhaps be illuminating of this orientation, or appear illuminated by it. If a critic should say: 'Yes, you are perhaps right that it is possible to see Western rationalism as one of the world's religious traditions; but so what?', perhaps these items, however skeletal, may prove suggestive of a possible answer.

First is the relation throughout Western history between what the West has called religion, on the one hand—the Christian, or Judaeo-Christian, heritage—and, on the other hand, this intellectualist/humanist tradition of which we have here been speaking. These two have, as we have said, proceeded sometimes in conflict, sometimes in harmony, often intertwined, but never quite fused. It has been standard to take note of their interrelation chiefly in terms of a polarity between faith and reason. The matter may be seen more truly, I suggest, as the historical development over the centuries of a relation between faith in God and faith in reason; or, finally, faith through the tradition from Palestine and faith through the tradition from Greece in Western culture.

To elaborate this perception would be a voluminous matter, obviously; I simply toss it out, though I may say that I personally have found it exceedingly fruitful, and my hunch would be that over the next many years this way of re-considering the issues involved will prove trenchant.

My second point is one instance of a ramification of the first. It is the suggestion that much of what is happening around us these days can be significantly interpreted on this basis.

For the force of our contention is, unfortunately, made more vivid in our day, in that faith through this tradition, as much if not more even than faith through the Christian or Jewish traditions, is in the Western world in danger of being lost. Many artists and novelists and thinkers, let alone men and women in the street, have lost not only faith in God, but faith in reason, a faith in the human. They see behind the flux of phenomena neither an ultimate person, creator, redeemer, judge, nor a rational order, a significant cosmic structure in relation to which, and in terms of which, meaning for human life can be apprehended and formulated. The loss of faith in reason (in the technical sense of faith and the classical sense of reason) is the real crisis of our universities and of our school system.

The loss of faith in *both* of the forms in which the West has known it (through the tradition from Palestine and through the tradition from Greece) is the crisis of our civilization.

Thirdly: modern philosophers of a certain type are to be found these days claiming that classical Western metaphysics was an intellectual error. Some linguistic analysts would even say, 'meaningless'. This otherwise odd fact can best be understood as paralleling the feeling among traditional Christians, and also among old-fashioned Western secularists, that Islamic, Hindu, and other religious positions were simply 'wrong'; sometimes also, 'meaningless nonsense'. In these latter cases many nowadays see such attitudes as parochial; and Christian theologians are beginning to wrestle valiantly with pluralism. The 'secular'-academic wing of our culture has yet to enter this phase wholeheartedly. Manifestly, for a long time, each religious symbol-system tended to make sense only to those who had faith in it (I would say: through it), and to appear absurd, even grotesque, to outsiders. To-day, however, we know that we must move beyond this. A modern thinker who does not understand classical Western metaphysics (whether approvingly or not), or finds it meaningless, is like a fundamentalist Christian who thinks Hindu or Islamic theology ridiculous.

Fourthly: my colleague at Harvard, the Professor of Sanskrit, recently formulated a question on a doctoral examination in Hinduism: 'Indian philosophy set the intellect on a much lower plane than did the Greek philosophers or, following them, the Christians. Choose two or three Indian systems of thought and show where they provide room for what has been called *nous*: mind, intellect, or the rational soul in the West. Speculate briefly on why the Indian evaluation should have differed from the European.' I have no idea what the students answered, or what the professor expected, here; but the question itself is significant. One need hardly add, I suppose, that Indian philosophical and metaphysical thought is at least as subtle, as refined, as complex, and as intelligent, as is Greek. At issue here is not the finesse of the respective systems, but the role perceived for Reason.

Fifth point: Westerners have never been able to decide whether what they have called 'Confucianism' is a religion or a philosophy. Sometimes the matter gets uncouthly worded as: 'Confucianism is not a religion, it is a philosophy.' My own formulation would be that the Confucian tradition in China, although different from both, is in some ways more like one of our Western traditions than it is like the other. (Yet in fact it resembles both significantly, and it is undiscerning to fail to appreciate its spiritual quality.) Germane here also is the fact that in the Hindu instance, any attempt to discriminate between 'religion' and 'philosophy' is inept. Philosophy in India has been Hindu (or Buddhist or Jain). In the past, Westerners who have approached the Indian scene assuming philosophy and religion to be two quite different things, have found this awkward. With our new orientation, both the Chinese and the Indian situations become for the first time fully intelligible.

Sixth: the faith of scientists. I mean their faith in science—in the spirit of science: in science not as an objective actuality in disparate parts, but as an elusive and integral dynamic of which the outward expressions at any given moment, although worthy, are always and in principle inadequate and to be superseded; a dynamic that is both demanding and rewarding; in which at their best they have delighted to be involved, and in which their involvement has given meaning to their work and even in some degree to their life. This faith has undergirded and informed and elicited and transcended their work. Their beliefs (the concrete parts of the specific sciences of the day) come and go; but their faith, with all its ultimate ineffability, persists. As long as it persists, the scientific tradition will creatively flourish; what would be the meaning and contour of a dying of that faith it is hard to say, though obviously it could die.

I suggest that it is metaphorical, but perhaps not misleading, to envisage Western science as an innovative and radical sect of the Greek rationalist tradition. Clearly it is in part derived from, and in part is in rebellion against, that tradition; a reformation at times stridently protestant.

Admittedly, many more scientists to-day than a generation or three ago, like many academics in general, are not in pursuit of truth so much as in pursuit of research grants; they aim not at the life of reason, so much as the advancement of their careers. (The explicitly religious institutions have faced this problem at times, when they were socially powerful.) It is my impression that the best scientists are still to-day more likely to be persons of faith (in truth, in a transcendent order of the cosmos) than are the routine ones; though there are exceptions. The loss of faith portends much.

Seventh: in the trilogue in Mediaeval Spain, when Jewish, Muslim, and Christian thinkers conversed together, it was the Aristotelian-based common 'faith' in reason that enabled them to do so. They were able to meet as common participants in the community formed around that tradition. A Chinese or an Indian intellectual at the time would not have been able to join in, even though he or she were just as intelligent and just as rational. This negative point is illustrated from the then contemporary situation in India, where Muslims and Hindus intermingled, but were able to establish a dialogue, insofar as they were able to do so at all, not on the basis of reason—although there were men and women of superb intelligence and high rationality on both sides; yet their rationalities diverged in form—but rather on the basis, in that case, of a common mystic orientation. Those on each side who did not share this maintained no dialogue. And while through Spain the common form that emerged was scholastic—with Islamic, Jewish, and Christian scholasticisms as varieties of that species—in India the common form that developed was mystical (*Bhakti* and *Sufi*).

This historical incident in Spain has also undergirded the dubious yet firm conviction among many in the West that reason in the Western sense is universal and unites humankind while religion (in the Western sense) is particular and divides. Fissiparous tendencies in human affairs are many and powerful; but are not so simple.

Eighth: traditionally, the West has had philosophy of religion. This has at times been philosophers' looking out upon what have been called the religions, and reporting back on what they see. It has largely been the assessment by adherents of the Western rationalist tradition, from within their perspective, of the other, more explicitly religious, traditions of humankind, known more or less widely, more or less deeply. This philosophizing about religion—in the sense of an interpretation from within the rationalist faith of other forms of faith—has had some sort of counterpart in the recent move in the Church to come up with a Christian 'theology of the religions': an interpretation in Christian terms, by and for Christians, of other groups' faith. My present paper might in a sense appear as a suggestion to turn the tables on the former: by constructing, instead of a philosophy of religion, rather a 'religion of philosophy'. More egalitarianly, rather, I am suggesting that we have no Archimedean point. Our study must be collaborative. We must move beyond an interpretation from one perspective out on the others, to a human interpretation of all.

Ninth: although the thesis here developed has, as pointed out, on occasion been adumbrated by, and is not therefore unfamiliar among, Western classical scholars, to many in other departments of modern academia it will appear surprising. Before, however, the science/religion controversy of last century and before the Enlightenment critique of religion, the affinities here propounded did not always seem remote. Some philosophers have rejected the so-called religions as irrational and bad; others have patronized them as approximations to rationality and therefore stepping-stones, as it were, on our way to truth. Comparably, many a classical Christian theologian has seen *philosophia* as a stepping-stone to Christian faith. Similarly while the early Christian missionaries in India, for instance, rejected 'Hinduism' as non-divine and bad, later more liberal ones patronized it as partial truth, to be fulfilled in Christianity. Early this century J.N. Farquhar, for example, wrote a book important for this 'fulfillment' theory, which he entitled *The Crown of Hinduism*, setting forth Christian faith as that crown; and various Indian Church and missionary thinkers discuss whether the Upanishads might be accepted as the Indian Christians' Old Testament. The point to be made here is that not only, except for Marcion, did the classical Christian thinkers do this for the Jewish tradition, making the Hebrew Bible an Old Testament to the Christian New; but that some did it also with the Greek. Clement of Alexandria, for instance, says that *philosophia* may be seen as having been given to the Greeks as the Law was given to the Jews, as their Old Testament;[15] and this sentiment was echoed, for instance, a millennium and a half later by Schleiermacher.[16]

Similarly, on the other side, Hegel might, I suppose, be instanced as a philosopher for whom the religious complexes of the world, and particularly the Christian, are as it were Old Testaments in the historical course of Reason's unfolding of itself towards the final chapter of its self-statement in philosophy.

Tenth, and finally: we end with a return to that business in China of a person's participating in, or finding faith through, two or more traditions at the same time; and the counterpart situation that we are proposing for the Westerner. I do not use the word 'faith' in the plural (just as I do not pluralize 'courage'); but would speak of two forms of faith, or faith mediated through, nurtured by, expressed in, two traditions. Western history has its two major traditions. Individuals who have been exposed to both have only exceptionally rejected either one. Although sometimes torn between them, and sometimes holding them in parallel, or juxtaposed, yet often they have integrated them—if not fully, at least as fully as many human beings often can integrate just one, or can find integrity for themselves through just one. The lives of most Westerners have been what they have been, it would be easy to contend, because of a combination in those lives of a contribution from, interaction with, the Graeco-Roman tradition on the one hand and the Judaeo-Christian on the other. More specifically there have been Christian intellectuals, of whom I suppose Aquinas has been the paradigm, and Jewish, of whom Maimonides—there have been many thousands of lesser instances, including a good number among one's personal friends. In China there have been, classically, three main traditions for everyman; in the West, two.

In conclusion: I am not saying that Greek *philosophia* is 'a religion'. For me, as I have argued in *The Meaning & End* . . . , there are no 'religions'. To be religious is a function of persons, not of things. These latter constitute traditions which are the evidence of, and the occasion for, the ordering of human lives in terms of inner and outer wholeness.

I am saying that the tradition stemming from Greece has made available to persons and groups, as have in differing ways the various explicitly religious traditions of our planet, a complex of ideas and even institutions in terms of which we could choose, or be given the grace, to live lives of faith—of coherence, dignity, meaning, in saving relation to ultimacy. For those who accept a religious awareness of transcendence, I would urge that *philosophia* has made available on earth one of the major ways by which that transcendence has entered human history, or men and women have touched the hem of the garment of transcendent truth. For those, on the other hand, whose sympathies are on the other side of the Western duality, I would argue that our religious systems can be more truly apprehended when discerned as comparable phenomena to that very loyalty to and pursuit of truth and understanding in which they themselves are involved. For my thesis, that *philosophia* is most truly to be viewed as one of the world's major religious traditions, holds that seeing it so illuminates not only that *philosophia* but also those other systems, and also—and most significantly—illumines the human in itself.

The university is the central focus of the Greek legacy in our culture. And the academic contribution to the understanding both of the human and of the religious is the recognition that these are not two categories, with human nature fundamentally secular and religion as some contingent additive, to be explained, even rationally explained; but rather one category in many forms—so that our rationalist heritage may enable us to understand our common humanity in its multiformity. Such understanding is self-understanding. The study of Comparative Religion is for the intellectual finally an exercise in self-consciousness, corporate and indeed global. In the endeavour to interpret the religious history of humankind, we have arrived at a point where each may recognize that 'I am studying not them but us'.

CHAPTER 4

On Mistranslated Booktitles

Of the pungent aphorism *traduttori traditori*, one of the inherent delights is that the phrase itself cannot be translated into other languages without betrayal; at the least, of its pithy charm. All language is imperfect, a reader (or hearer) always understanding what is said in a way that leaves out something of what the writer (or speaker) means, and a way that adds something of what the reader (or hearer) supposes, or imposes, Ortega y Gasset has thoughtfully argued.[1] I agree with this, yet hold that this characteristic of the human situation need not dishearten. We do better to marvel at how much the written or spoken word succeeds in communicating among persons—succeeds in building community between and among persons—than to bemoan that it does not succeed flawlessly.

Moreover, sometimes one can learn from the very flaws.

Translating, in turn, need not redouble this fallibility of human understanding; although it may nicely illustrate it. In particular, its flaws can provide a lucid chance to learn. What we read in, what we leave out, may become visible or at least open to study, once what we have grasped of an expression appears and is fixed in quite another vocabulary. The historian of ideas is well served by translations. Especially major works of thought, and particularly when rendered in a different century as well as a different language from the original, may function as rich and firm documentation for even quite subtle shifts in conceptual and perceptual habits.

My purpose in this present essay is to call attention to two or three widely used English translations of salient books in the field of religious thought, whose titles, I suggest, contain sufficient error to be illuminating. They illuminate not merely specific misunderstanding, but the general history of ideas. Titles are chosen because pivotal. When a book becomes famous, its title encapsulates for many what is sensed as its message. If the title be wrong (that is, wrongly worded) it distorts—significantly, I propose. We shall focus on Schleiermacher's *The Christian Faith*, but first note in passing two others, leading into my main argument by proffering additional and rather different instances of my general point.[2]

We begin with Durkheim.

In English, from the noun 'element' two adjectives are formed: 'elemental' and 'elementary'. Their meanings are distinct, the former signifying what pertains to or is one of the constituent parts or basic components, while the latter implies rudimentary, incipient. French, on the other hand, has but one: '*élémentaire*', serving both purposes. If one reflects on this matter, will one not conclude that *Les formes élémentaires de la vie religieuse*[3] was a work setting forth primarily a new thesis about the fundamental ingredients of which religious life is to be seen as constituted? 'Elemental', then, would have rendered this notion more accurately. The work is about the elements of humanity's religious life.

Nonetheless, the choice of 'elementary', although ultimately I would contend a mistranslation, was by no means stupid. Joseph Ward Swain knew French well, and understood the subject matter well, no doubt. There were reasons—one might even wish to say, compelling reasons—for his choice. First, Durkheim contended, explicitly in his opening pages, that the surest way to ascertain what are the 'constituent elements' (p. 3, also p. 7), the 'permanent [*sic*] elements' (p. 5) (*éléments constitutifs*—pp. 4, 9; *éléments permanents*—p. 6) of religion is to see them in a situation where they are uncomplicated, unmixed; as among Australian aboriginals. Secondly, at the turn of the century two views were widespread: that the nature of religion (and indeed of many other human and especially social matters) is manifested in its earliest forms; and that these long-ago forms of all religious (and social) life have been preserved virtually unchanged by present-day 'primitive' tribes (as the very word 'primitive' both indicates and consolidates).[4] The phrase 'the origin and nature of religion' (or vice versa) was current in those days, it being widely assumed that the two go together; that of course primitive religion is the key to all religion.

The two matters that I have noted here might be seen as essentially one, Durkheim's turning to Australian Bushmen for an elucidation of the elements of religion being but a particular illustration of the then general position. Yet I discriminate between them, since one need not have subscribed to the general theory in order to find Durkheim's particular thesis interesting. Specifically, I wonder whether a translator who rejected the general position, or even one who queried it, might not have been more likely than one who took it for granted, to opt rather for 'elemental' than for 'elementary' when faced in the Durkheim book with the choice that the French adjective *élémentaire* in principle poses for every anglophone. My basic submission is that the rendering of Durkheim's title as 'The Elementary Forms of Religious Life' illustrates the far from insignificant fact that the translation was made at a phase in Western cultural evolution when sophisticated secular intellectuals tended to hold that chronologically early and in its wake present-day tribal religious life was closer, or more manageably close, to the truth about religion generically than are our more developed forms.

In fact there was something of a struggle in universities in the era after Durkheim and Swain to have Comparative Religion as a serious academic study include primarily the 'great' or 'high' religious movements of the world, Hindu, Buddhist, and the rest, and not simply 'primitive' (which word has indeed had by now to be dropped). Ironically, some might even wish to suggest that the ways of Australian Bushmen as Durkheim depicts them do indeed illustrate the *elementary* forms of religious life, in the sense of an early stage of development, with that life since or elsewhere moving on to much greater and even innovative developments. Yet *that is not what Durkheim intended to say*. His work is a monument to the days when elementary was thought to be elemental, and vice versa. Swain's translation illustrates the misapprehension—and fixed it, contributing gratuitously to disseminating for a good while in the English-speaking world a major presupposition.

There is a range of alternative presuppositions, of course, and of ways of viewing the religious. One, for instance: just as some might see elementary education as minor compared to the more sophisticated education available at universities, and even this as an approximation to education ideally and in its true sense, so some would think of religion as merely adumbrated in tribal societies, more fully developed in 'the world religions', but still only imperfectly realized. A still different view would see the forms of religious life as differing from place to place and century to century, no one set of them being essential or elemental: that religion does not necessarily have an essence (or if it does, this does not lie in forms). And so on. Swain's translation helps us to place him—and helped its readers unconsciously to place themselves—in a particular stance.

Our second instance is Thomas Aquinas, *De Veritate Catholicae Fidei.*[5] It brings us closer to our final concern, Schleiermacher. In the Durkheim-Swain case, the presuppositions of the time were common to both author and translator, who were contemporaries, the latter making explicit in English what was, at most, implicit in French. In the Aquinas case, the twentieth-century rendering imposes on a text presuppositions that were quite absent in the thirteenth century when it was written, thus distorting more. Much had happened in the seven centuries between the writing of this work and its 1955 version in English[6] to which we shall attend.

Except for the first word (the preposition 'On'), every part of the title's modern rendering, 'On the Truth of the Catholic Faith' is misleading as to the content of the work, and yet instructive as to the modern outlook that receives it. The translators themselves, their minds steeped in the mediaeval thought-world, may have heard their English phrasing as signifying more or less what they knew the Latin to mean, without reflecting on the disparities from modern times and on the ineptitude of modern uncritical language to render them. To most others, however, the wording surely communicates a meaning, and a context for meaning, remote from those of the book being translated. *Veritas*, which mediaevally signified also 'reality' and 'genuineness', referred to 'truth' by no means in that sense of a starkly theoretical verbalized judgement that alone the word in English to-day connotes to many. How much more was included, Thomas's other great treatise *De Veritate* strongly elucidates.[7] Secondly: 'Catholic' in modern English—a language whose flavour and connotations have been set, of course, chiefly by Protestant usage and in a sociologically chiefly Protestant situation—when spelled with a capital C, is a term that to-day means to almost all who hear it, including Catholics themselves, 'Roman Catholic as distinct from Protestant'; in a way that Thomas cannot be imagined as understanding, let alone intending. 'Faith', I have been at pains to document historically in recent studies,[8] has changed its meaning drastically over the centuries to many who hear it (although I personally am engaged in a heavy struggle to rehabilitate its erstwhile connotation). There remains one word, tiny yet insidious. Equally telling is the decision (arbitrary?—probably not thought out carefully, in any case) to introduce the definite article in English—a transformation that coheres with, and strongly corroborates, the innovatively contemporary rather than the traditional dimensions of the implications of the other words in the title insofar as these are still ambiguous.

Unlike most other European languages, English has (i) generic nouns used without an article ('butter', 'courage', 'paper', 'piety' . . .) and only in the singular, and (ii) concrete nouns used in the singular with an article, with a plural always available either with the definite article or with none ('the box', 'the papers', 'a goddess', 'civilizations' . . .). 'Faith' used to be a generic. Thomas explicitly affirms it to be 'one', not multiple;[9] and conservative modern Christian theologians refuse to this day (as also do I) to accept the neologism 'faiths' as though there were or could be more than one; as though it were concrete, not generic; an object, not a quality; more like a doctrine or an overcoat than like courage or piety. Whenever a plural exists, its singular presumes the article, definite or indefinite; and vice versa. To speak of *the* Christian faith, or the Islamic, the Buddhist, or to speak of the true faith (over against false or imperfect or partial ones?) is to take one's place in the modern outlook which sees faiths as (mundane?) objects of various kinds. 'The Catholic faith', as a phrase, presupposes for most hearers an entity specified as Roman Catholic and distinguished from the Jewish faith, the Hindu, the Protestant, and others. It is an objectifying response to modern pluralism (of which more below).

Not that Thomas was altogether unaware of what we call pluralism. On the whole his mind worked entirely within Christian horizons; yet this particular book, which after his death became known under an alternative and somewhat spurious title, *Summa Contra Gentiles*, was, exceptionally, written in response to a request from his fellow Dominican nearer the frontiers of Christendom both geographically and intellectually, and more aware than was he of intelligent people who were not Christian: Raymond of Peñafort.[10] Yet he was quite explicitly not writing of Christian faith as distinct from other forms of faith; let alone, not of the

Christian (or the Catholic) as distinct from other faiths. For him, outsiders did not have aberrant faith; they were, rather, bereft of faith. The subtitle of his treatise is *contra errores infidelium*, 'against the aberrations of those who are *without faith*'. That non-Christians had faith—or faiths—but of some other sort, was an idea of which he was innocent.

Yet does the use of an adjective not move some distance towards specifying, even if not so far as to legitimize, the definite article? This particular adjective, however, is the contrary of specific. (Even to-day, 'Christian courage' or 'Christian piety' does not imply that the speaker is thinking of a series of courages or pieties and is specifying one in such a series.) I have elsewhere commented on Thomas's rare use of *christiana fides*;[11] and it is hardly far-fetched to see him here propounding the thesis that faith is universal (*catholica*) and therefore is apt for all persons wherever and whoever they be—be they Moors or whatever. He was aware of faith in what we to-day cannot but call only one of its series of forms: namely, that linked with the Christian Church. Accordingly he saw that form as universal—in theory, as all his work shows; and as this work shows, potentially also in practice. (Besides, it could be argued that in his usage the phrase signifies 'faith in Christ'.)[12]

Crucial for the translating project, next, is the relation between *fides* and *veritas*, expressed in the Latin by a genitive (the only way in Latin of directly relating two nouns). The modern English rendering of the title reflects, or at least lends itself to promoting, the present-day tendency to presuppose that faiths are true or false, primarily even in the sense of being equivalent to or inextricably associated with propositions, to which those adjectives then may apply. Does the phrasing 'the truth of the Catholic faith' not communicate to most modern readers the notion (of a subjective genitive, as the grammarians say) that this particular faith is being adjudged to be true; and to the majority, in the further sense that its beliefs are correct? That is not what the Latin title affirms. A minority, perhaps, would hear the English, somewhat more traditionally, as signifying that this particular faith is true in the sense, rather, of being genuine or authentic (not spurious or phoney). (Compare 'true courage', 'a true marriage'.) In either case, however—given the use of the definite article—the implication would be virtually inescapable that concomitantly some faith, or even that some faiths, is or are false. Thomas could not conceive such a thing. False faith was not one of his conceptual categories.[13] He wrote at length on faith: for him, the term designates a God-given good, and nothing else.

Rather, in the original title, the notion is that the[14] faith under discussion acknowledges something that is genuinely there. We can be confident of this because, as I have had occasion to note elsewhere,[15] the author in his opening paragraphs is in fact quite explicit as to the purpose of the book: namely (not to argue that a particular faith, or even a particular form of faith, or even faith generically, is true; but rather) to make manifest the reality (or: the truth) that such faith professes.[16] A counterpart is his *veritas rationis*, which the translators render as 'the truth of reason'. This does not signify that reason—let alone, not that one particular reason as distinct from others—is not false but true. Rather, explicitly, it refers to that truth, that reality, to which reason has or gives access—which he formally correlates with that to which faith does.[17]

'The truth of faith' (*veritas fidei*), thus, is not its validity, certainly not its intellectual correctness; but rather, the reality to which it relates.

That reality is God: *prima veritas* of which Thomas regularly speaks.

The whole title, therefore, means something on the order of: 'On the reality of that to which faith generically is oriented'. Certainly some such phrasing approximates his position more closely than what is signified to most hearers by 'On the truth of the Catholic faith'.

This last, however—to return to the argument of this paper—though on scrutiny a mistake in translation, is an instructive one. An historian of ideas could readily discern in what phase of the evolution of anglophone culture it was produced; and could use it to illustrate the ideological transition through which its wording shows those involved to have been going, and the implicit presuppositions for which that wording is evidence.

We turn finally to Schleiermacher, and to the English translation (1928) of his great and influential work *Der christliche Glaube*. (The German was originally published in 1821; a second edition, the one later translated, appeared in 1830.)[18] It is my contention, which I hope herein to prove, that the English title *The Christian Faith*[19] is in fact a mistranslation: a subtle one yet highly significant and, alas, influential. It will become clear also that the error is not only readily understandable, but instructive for understanding the transitions in religious thought that characterize the century lying between the two versions—and specifically, the reifying process that the English phrasing embodied, and by so doing helped to perpetuate and to strengthen. One result is that the present growing awareness that reification is distorting, and present endeavours to conceptualize more fruitfully and to theologize more constructively, tend in the English-speaking world to appear, often unconsciously, to have Schleiermacher not as an ally but to some degree as an obstacle.

Schleiermacher is important in the history of Christian thought in, of course, many ways. The two that concern us here are that he stands at the beginning of the major new phase of Western intellectual, and social, development characterized by two novel orientations in matters pertaining to the consciousness of faith: (i) a sharp differentiating between something now being called 'religion' and the rest of culture (phrased, even, as between religion and culture *simpliciter*), and (ii) pluralism. The former, the religion/culture polarity, has had to do primarily with the modern West, but has since been imposed on the rest of the world. The latter, pluralism, has to do primarily with our incipient global awareness, but was quickly applied also at home, specifically in a new recognition by Christians of the faith of Jews (of faith among Jews).

On the former matter, Schleiermacher produced the first work ever written explicitly on religion simply as such. His lectures *Über die Religion*[20] constitute, it would seem, the first book in all of human history on religion as a great something: a distinguishable and in some sense separate matter in human affairs, to be considered in and of itself. Two comments may be made on this, too. The first is that the work is apologetics (as the subtitle confirms): the new conception emerging among disparaging outsiders is here being derivatively assimilated by the insider, in a not at all unwonted pattern.[21] From its critics, Schleiermacher accepted 'religion' as a generic. Secondly, and of special interest to us here, is that the English translation translates this accurately, as a generic:

On Religion (1893).[22] It is not rendered as 'On the Religion', of course, which would not make sense (would be bad grammar). The definite article in English is reserved, as always, for the concrete rather than the generic noun, the former having its plural. *Die Religion und die Religionen* is 'Religion and the Religions'. This phrase, with its two articles in German, one in English, in accord with the structure of each language, became the rubric for a theoretical issue of some moment: to explore the relation between the generic and the particular, the various particulars.[23]

On this pluralism issue, Schleiermacher has the distinction of being also the first Christian thinker in history to write a theology explicitly considering the Christian as one among several modes of faith (*Glaubensweisen*, as he dynamically worded it). He was not, as for a time I imagined the case to be, the first Christian theologian, but rather the second, to write specifically on 'Christian theology' rather than on theology *simpliciter*. Virtually all previous Christian thinkers took for granted—as we have seen Thomas Aquinas doing, and as many still do—that such specification would be otiose. (It was only in the 1960s that Harvard University changed the name of its Ph.D. degree in this subject from 'Theology' to 'Christian Theology', on my initiative on joining its faculty; few institutions have thought of following suit. I am one of perhaps relatively few persons who have taught both Christian theology and Islamic theology—which has helped perhaps to push me towards an aiming at generic 'world' theology.)[24]

Schleiermacher's sole predecessor in this particular matter is Abelard, one of whose works is entitled *Theologia christiana*[25]—the only instance before the nineteenth century where such a qualification is enshrined in a title, so far as I have been able to discover. I do not know enough mediaeval history to understand whether his aberration here was related to his sense of Platonic and other Greek and even Jewish theologizing as alternate types, or related to the subsequent ecclesiastical condemnation of his thought at the Council of Sens in 1140.

In any case, Abelard's innovation had few on-going consequences; Schleiermacher's, seven hundred years later, has rightly had many. Although some of us have bemoaned the slowness with which Christian theologians have addressed themselves in full seriousness to the pluralism issue—most have been too busy fighting rear-guard actions against Western secularist thought—they are to-day beginning to turn their attention to this matter; and for long it has been, though not central, at least a minor background element in the consciousness or the subconscious of many of those who write, or anyway those who read, (Christian) theology.

Any Christian theologian has nowadays to take a position self-consciously on issues that in the past were not articulated. In particular, on the pluralism question we may delineate three options. Does he or she regard the faith that Christians have (have been given) as *sui generis*, other communities having not faith but something else; or is faith a more or less universal generic, of which the Christian is one form (or mode), or of which there are various Christian forms, and as well there are Islamic, Buddhist, Jewish, and other forms also; or are there different 'faiths', the Christian faith, the Hindu faith, the Shinto faith, and so on, varying autonomous instances (perhaps drastically diverse) of a single genus?

Of these three, the first has been the view recently of many Barthians: 'they have religions, we have faith'.[26] Earlier, this was the standard Christian position, as the word 'infidel' for non-Christians clarifies, and as we saw with Thomas. The third—'faiths' as a plural, or with the definite article: 'the Christian faith', 'the Buddhist faith', 'they have not kept the faith intact', 'people of different faiths' . . .—has arisen from an unreflective attempt to correct the ignorance and arrogance of this, and is a prevalent view. It is adopted also, often casually, by a number of Christian theologians who have not thought it through, indeed have not thought about the matter much and do not know (or care?) a great deal about other religious communities. The second—'faith' as a generic, a universal human quality appearing in different forms—is a position that I personally have of late written rather extensively to advocate,[27] contending that it alone can do justice to the facts either of Christian history and experience or of others', let alone both. Whichever position, however, one may oneself adopt, or however one might defer choosing, it is possible historically to determine what stand major thinkers in the past have in fact taken; and to note their arguments or assumptions.

There would seem no question but that Schleiermacher's position was expressly the second of our three. We know this, from a variety of indications: most conspicuously, from his quite explicitly saying so. He was at pains to spell out his careful reasons for rejecting the position of those who fail to see 'the homogeneity of all these products of the human spirit' (*in allen diesen Erzeugnissen des menschlichen Geistes die Gleichartigkeit*).[28] Indeed, he devotes the second of the four substantial parts of his opening chapter to arguing expressly for continuity among the world's religious groups, low or high.[29]

At stake are momentous issues. Anti-religious or irreligious people, firm secularists who deny a transcendent reality to which what the West has called faith is the appropriate human orientation and response, tend of course to the positivist third of our three options. Indeed it was they who generated it; and their outlook that underlies its inherent disparagement, its reductionism. (Modern atomism, of course, has helped.) Within their particular ideology it makes good sense. For others, however—for anyone who takes faith as valid, not deceptive, not a great human error; for serious theologians, presumably—it is finally incoherent. Schleiermacher is not insensitive to this. Our particular interest here is, however, not his general position but the phrasing in which he repeatedly sets it forth, quietly yet forcefully. If heeded, these subtler instances evinced in his use of language make manifest his view as surely as do the more direct statements; and to translate them otherwise is to distort.

Let us consider, then, how he uses the term *der Glaube*; and how his translators render it. The whole book, of course, is an exposition of his understanding as to what constitutes this quality. One may go further, and say that the whole book, except the Introduction, sets forth a thesis about faith in its Christian 'mode'; as we have noted, the Introduction is concerned with that particularity, but thereafter it is simply taken as given that the topic is faith among Christians. Our concern here is simply the question as to whether he treats it as generic or particular: and therefore, whether in English the term should appear without, or with, an article. Our first observation is that throughout the remainder of the book, the translators evidently render his *der Glaube* simply as 'faith'.[30] The second observation is that in the Introduction also, with its discussion of the relation of the Christian to other instances, forms or modes of faith, the same is usually true.[31] (Where 'the faith' occurs in English [§10:68/47], it turns out to be a translation not of *der Glaube* but of *die Glaubensweise*.) Even the sparsely used phrase *der christliche Glaube* is rendered once as 'Christian faith', generically.[32] The particularizing 'the Christian faith' does not seem to appear in the English, except in the book's title. (Might it almost seem that the translators when constrained by the specific contexts of Schleiermacher's thought, in rendering his sentences and paragraphs, apprehended his meaning for this phrase as generic, and only in the title of the work, freed from all context, did their unconscious particularizing instincts fully win out?)

Strikingly, he never uses *Glaube* in the plural.[33] (The Germans generally still do not.) His English translators betray him: they do use 'faiths'. As we have suggested, they speak (present him as speaking) of 'Christian piety' and other, different, 'forms of piety' (no article in the former and no plural for the generic in the latter);[34] in contrast, their recurrent 'other faiths' renders his *andere Glaubensweisen*.[35] Similarly, their wording 'a monotheistic faith' (with the indefinite article), 'any particular faith', turn out on inquiry to be their substitution for his *eine . . . monotheistische Glaubensweise* and *eine Glaubensweise* respectively.[36] They speak of 'the actual historical faiths', where he has *die geschichtlich vorkommenden Glaubensweisen* (§9:62/42). When they refer to 'an adherent of some other faith', it turns out that they are rendering his *ein fremder Glaubensgenosse* (§11:83/59). In similar vein, on occasion (though this is not standard with them) they proffer 'religions' to their English reader where he has written, rather, *Gestaltungen [der] Frömmigkeit*.[37] Comparably, *die christliche Frömmigkeit* is turned into 'the Christian religion' with the definite article; although they follow this with '(piety)' in parentheses, without indicating what the reader is expected to do with that definite article in this alternative.[38] (By 1928 'piety' had not yet been reified, and still is generally not, even though 'religion' and 'faith' had widely been.) 'Every individual religion' is their reified form of his *jede eigentümliche Glaubensweise*.[39]

And so on. The several dozen instances that one may collect show on the one hand that the English translation is sometimes quietly faithful to the generic original; and on the other hand that wherever it does present this author as thinking and writing in terms of a series of distinct religions, or individual faiths, a comparison with the original makes it evident that in fact in every single case without exception he has thought and written in line with his continuity thesis, with his conviction that all the various instances of piety across the world are lower or higher forms of, modes of, the one universal human characteristic that is faith.[40] He is quite clear that for him the Christian is the highest and purest of these various modes;[41] and he explicitly presumes that all Christians share that judgement.[42] Yet he nowhere uses language appropriate to a view, which indeed he consciously rejects, that there are many faiths.

This view, on the other hand, his English translators *unconsciously* accept. Presupposing that stance, they misrepresent him too as holding it; as writing in terms of it. Their version offers him to the English-reading public as one whose mind operates within that different outlook. Their language (and accordingly, what they present as his thought) at many points both presupposes and perpetuates, binds Schleiermacher to and makes his work serve the cause of, a theological interpretation of our human pluralist situation alien to his mind and heart.

We turn then to his title. A close reading of his long opening chapter in German, and a collation of his phrasings with theirs, makes it, I submit, beyond cavil that his book is about the Christian instance of faith generically. I submit, therefore, that the more accurate rendition of its title would be *Christian Faith*. By introducing the article, by calling it *The Christian Faith*, they illustrate the insensitivity of our century to issues that to Schleiermacher were fundamental. They even thereby helped to desensitize us to those issues, so that some to-day hardly appreciate the difference; hardly recognize what an egregious error theirs was.

So effective was their skewing of a vision!

The real problem, however, is not that certain scholars misread a German text. The significant point is rather that their wording illustrates how a certain era has misread the human religious situation.

CHAPTER 5

Shall Next Century be
Secular or Religious?

From the invitation to come to Japan to attend this gathering and to give this talk, I understood our topic to be a consideration of present-day intellectual trends in modernist enlightened circles, with special reference to religious concerns as perceived therein; and reflection on the likelihood that that perception next century will differ. I myself imagine, certainly I hope, that it will differ. When first asked to speak, therefore, I proposed as title for my talk, 'Will Next Century be Secular or Religious?' After a time I changed this, feeling diffident about pretentiousness in seeming to presume to predict the future on a global scale—something beyond human capacity. I therefore proposed instead 'Should Next Century be Secular or Religious?' The point of that change was that I have solid views, which you will be hearing in a moment—views that I am happy to set before you for your criticism and judgement—as to what is reasonable and would be seriously helpful in this realm; what would make for a better world. Again, however, it seemed pretentious to appear to be claiming that I am, or indeed any other merely human being is, in a position to pass a moral judgement on the future, or on humankind globally. Finally, therefore, I have modified the wording once again, to 'Shall Next Century be Secular or Religious?' The force of that phrasing, with a first-person-plural sense of joint self-involvement, is to put a question to you, as to whether the views that I propound are indeed sufficiently persuasive that you and I should take on the moral responsibility of hoping and striving that the situation as depicted come about. Is this way of envisaging the world reasonable and good, attractive intellectually and morally, so that we should jointly decide to move in this direction?

Thus, this new wording does not pretend to talk about the future absolutely; nor in relation to absolute moral standards.

Rather, it ventures to talk about it in relation to us. Theists among you will agree that only God knows either what will happen, on a global scale, after we die, or what should happen. Our inescapable task, however, is to think about it, responsibly, insofar as we are able to affect it.

Thus an advantage of the new wording is that it recognizes and incorporates a new fact that has arisen in our world: that we human beings have to decide what shape we are to try to give to our planet's future. There may not be a twenty-first century, if humanity acts in certain stupid and wicked ways; even in certain blind or short-sighted or narrow self-centred ways. The development of human history has become, for intellectuals, self-conscious; and for humankind as a whole increasingly self-directed— although still, of course, only partly so. How you and I answer the question 'Shall Next Century be Secular or Religious?' will affect the way that we personally think, and act, and are. That will affect the twenty-first century as a whole a little, even though only a little. It will affect us a lot.

My answer to the question, however we phrase it, is a probably unexpected one: namely, 'no'. Next century will not be either secular or else religious, nor indeed some combination of these, is my judgement and my aspiration. Let us hope, and strive, that it not be, is my invitation. I hesitate to affirm that the polarity between the two will not in fact last another hundred years. I feel that it should not last; but what I am saying for the moment is that we should not perpetuate it. We should think and feel and act not in terms of this either/or dichotomy. Rather, let us move beyond it to a newer, and truer, and more helpful, vision. That vision is nowadays possible, and, I suggest, attractive; indeed, compelling. I think that we should recognize, and should persuade our fellows, that it is not true, and not helpful, to imagine that everything and everyone is either secular or religious. We shall understand the world better, and become better persons, if we abandon these categories and use concepts that more truly grasp the reality in which we live, and the reality that we are. Let me explain.

What I am suggesting is that the terms 'secular' and 'religious' were pushed upon us by thinkers who understood the world, and the human condition within it, poorly, and that our endeavours to think by means of these terms has been proving misleading.

We must forge new concepts with which to analyse these matters; to understand better what we are and where we are going; and where we would do well to be going.

The universe is in motion. Everything that exists on earth, or that has ever existed, has come into existence historically, and has been always in process of transition. This is as true of ideas and conceptual frameworks, of words and languages, as it is of mountain ranges, continents, and galaxies as well as of clouds and international exchange rates. Our awareness of the world evolves; as does also the way that we analyse and correlate such things as we are aware of. One of the most important new developments was the recent rise and widespread establishment in especially the 19th century of the notion 'secularism', and that of the various so-called 'religions' of the world, and the idea that 'religious' and 'secular' are alternatives, between which one chooses. The term 'humanism' also emerged in the 19th century, as part of that era's great move to objectivize. European roots for these developments can of course be traced much further back. The new growth was, however, substantially different from those roots.

Japanese civilization over the centuries has been developed on the basis of two originally separate traditions, one indigenous, your own distinctive Japanese culture, the other from the mainland, specifically China. The dynamic interplay of the two has led to an on-going succession of entrancing patterns. Sometimes the two have been received as complementary, sometimes they have been in interesting tension, sometimes they have seemed to be virtually fused. More recently, a further tradition has been brought in, from the modern West. You seem to have made more progress towards integrating also it than probably any other people on earth. (The West itself, some would say, is doing perhaps less well, and anyway apparently no better, at integrating its cultural heritage with its own modernity.) In a teasingly comparable way, there have been two originally separate strands of which Western civilization has been woven: the tradition from Greece & Rome, the tradition from Palestine. These two have been sometimes harmonized, sometimes in conflict; sometimes intertwining, sometimes juxtaposed; but never fused. The polarity between 'secular' and 'religious' arose in the West signifying a divergence between the two: naming them, with the implication that they belonged to two different species.

The term 'secularism' was coined in 1851, and became popular at a time when the relation of the West's two traditions was largely conflict; at a time, also, when religious pluralism was not yet an everyday affair, was not yet much in people's minds. (The rest of the world has been familiar with diversity of so-called 'religious' traditions for millennia, but the West has been becoming so only very recently.) At that point, then, to Westerners 'religious' meant Christian, and 'secular' meant Graeco-Roman idealism: two spiritual traditions each of mighty power. The new polarity meant then that persons were being invited to choose between two spiritual movements that the European Enlightenment had seen as incompatible. Many even of those unwilling to make the either/or choice, unwilling to see the two as incompatible, nonetheless accepted the idea that they were, and should be, separated; certainly in society, and even at times in personal life.

In fact, however, both traditions were oriented on the one hand to the world in which we live, and on the other to a transcendent vision, diversely conceived. Looking back from our wider perspective, we can now see that it was a conflict between particular world-views, both members of the same species. An historian of religion recognizes as not uncommon the emergence from time to time of such conflicts, sometimes rising to the point where they may be subsumed under the heading of 'religious wars'. Even short of conflict, it is quite standard that both what are called ideologies and what are called religions have felt, usually strongly, that what they themselves profess is simply a recognition of the way things are, whereas other positions are of a different sort, are human constructs distorting the truth. This is, of course, quite natural, and was well-nigh ubiquitous in a pre-pluralist age. It requires a high degree of sophistication to recognize that one's fundamental outlook is one among many possible ones, perhaps equally plausible. Presuppositions usually remain firmly 'pre-'. Christian and Islamic dismissal of other religious systems is notorious; but Marxism, Freudianism, feminism, and the like think of other outlooks, especially those that criticize them, as merely 'ideologies' or 'rationalizations' or 'as not yet raised consciousness', while their own positions are a faithful portrayal of reality. We shall look more closely in a moment at secularism's disparagement of what it dismissed as 'religion'.

By now two developments, both of them highly consequential, have changed this earlier situation. First, we have all become aware that visions of transcendence—and of the world—are indeed diversely conceived. The transcendent realm is in its full reality so beyond our minds' final grasp that all attempts to conceptualize it and to pattern human life in relation to it are approximations only— even though some of the approximations have proven exceedingly rich and powerful and enduring, as the religious and cultural history of the world strikingly attests. Those of you in the Far East have long since recognized that there is merit in giving heed to more than one of the traditional systems of teachings that have been inherited; whereas the West has been rather fiercely monopolistic in this matter, insisting that one must be either a Christian or a Buddhist, for example, but not both; either a Jew or a Taoist. Through most of its history, however, the West has made an exception for the Graeco-Roman tradition. Christian humanism, for instance (using 'humanism' in its classical humanist sense) has been explicitly advocated; and thinkers like Aquinas and Maimonides are but outstanding examples illustrating the convergence, while in fact there have been millions of lesser folk who have deliberately or unconsciously been influenced, indeed moulded, by both the West's great legacies. Actually, virtually all Western civilization until the 19th century participated, and most of it still participates, in both traditions—to varying degrees, consciously and unconsciously.

'Secularism' as a concept, however, as I have indicated, was developed precisely to single out one side of this inheritance and to advocate the view that we should align ourselves with only one, not both, of the two movements. Similarly, as noted above, the concept 'humanism' to refer to that position began to be used during the latter half of the nineteenth century, with of course a major contribution from Auguste Comte and his phrase 'the religion of humanity'; but it was only at the beginning of this century that the word was put forth explicitly to become a firm alternative—by now to all forms of transcendentalism, theist or other.[1] Since the European Enlightenment was largely deist, though not theist, humanism as a godless vision is chiefly twentieth-century. Even then it was for a while idealistic.

The other major development that has profoundly affected the new situation has been even more consequential. It has been the de-transcendentalizing of that secular-humanist wing of Western civilization. Since the rest of the world has been influenced by this largely in its detranscendentalized form, this has been doubly important. Within the West, the devastation is becoming massive.

This loss of transcendence is crucial. Let me explain a little what I mean. I have remarked that transcendence is diversely conceived by the human mind; and diversely expressed in other social and individual forms. That is quite straightforward, since part of what we mean by transcendence is that it transcends—goes beyond—our full grasp. Yet although we cannot comprehend it, we can apprehend it. And we do. Part of what it means to be human is that we are normally aware of a reality that transcends not only us but all that we see or know. I will develop this point presently. Meanwhile, I wish simply to insist that in their classical form both secularism and humanism were movements that used to inculcate not merely an acknowledgement of, but a commitment to an active pursuit of, transcending ideals. Justice is one such transcendent ideal: something only partly actual but beckoning, demanding our allegiance and rewarding to pursue; let alone, to realize. One strives to discern it, and discerning is important, though never complete: in the world one will never actualize it fully, but it can be attained in larger measure than is currently the case, and that would be greatly worthwhile, and worth sacrifice and persisting struggle. Truth was another of the transcendent ideals. Universities in Europe were originally Christian institutions, then became increasingly 'secular' but for long this did not mean that they had abandoned the search for truth. On the contrary, they held, and proclaimed, that truth is an ever elusive yet ever demanding goal, enormously rewarding both those who seek it and those who find it, however partial the intermediate truth that is all that one ever finds. Rationalism, also, affirmed not that all human beings are in fact reasonable but that we are capable of being so (lack of that capacity being a pitiable and strange disease, called madness). It affirmed further that Reason, often out of reverence spelled with a capital R, is transcendently given, and self-subsistent; that the universe is rational, and that human beings are potentially rational, and therefore can understand the universe; or, put more carefully, can move towards an ever increasing understanding of it; and that our lives can be lived rationally, and should be; our societies can be organized rationally, and should be. To use our minds rationally and to behave rationally are again not only morally imperative but enormously bountiful: requiring our loyalty, and richly rewarding it. Reason could give us each individually personal dignity and worth, and enable us to live together socially in concord and success.

'Humanism' itself was an idealist, not an empirical, concept. In Greek metaphysical fashion, it postulated humanity as an ideal, to which actual persons only approximate, but which it is our duty, and our reward, to approximate ever more closely. It preached not that we human beings all already are humanist in its understanding of the term, in actual practice, but that we ought to become so; that we are so in principle, and it would be better if we became so in fact. This constitutes a striking contradiction in terms, unless one presupposes the metaphysical idealism underlying it. To believe in what humanity may and should, one discerns, ideally become, but not to be content with what and how we in practice are, with the human scene as empirically extant, is to postulate an ultimate loyalty to transcendence.

All this has been in process of changing. In the Modern West, not only Christian and Jewish visions have been recently rejected by many intellectuals, but also Greek metaphysics. What is significant is that not only these formulations of an awareness of the transcendence that surrounds us, beckoning, commanding, rewarding, have been abandoned; but that awareness itself. The sense that we live in a universe whose final reality is higher than we but with which we are in touch, has waned. This sense was previously well-nigh universal throughout humankind, even though it has been articulated in differing ways. Each tradition, being finite, has at its best drawn attention to certain facets of the transcendence to which humanity is open, and emphasized these; and has expressed them in particular—if you like, in symbolic—ways. Yet the particular ways that traditionally symbolized it have for many ceased to prove effective. Although the transcendence of course remains, human awareness of it and ability to live in terms of it have been seriously weakened.

The humanism that used to set before us a lofty though distant ideal of humanity that it was our humble duty to strive to rise to, and to subordinate ourselves to serve, has been largely replaced by a humanism that sees nothing valuable outside ourselves, so that it is our proud privilege to be self-assertive, subordinating everything to us.

In universities, those who were in pursuit of truth have to a significant extent been followed by those in pursuit of research grants, or of promotions. Truth itself, as the proclaimed goal of a university, has largely been reduced from something that we serve to something that serves us; from something to which we aspire to something that we construct. The academic enterprise then becomes the knowledge industry: the instrument by which a society turns out knowledge as it turns out motor cars, for consumption and for our own profit or pleasure or aggrandizement. Socrates's 'knowledge is virtue' has been widely replaced by Bacon's 'knowledge is power'. Rationalism in the sense of a disciplined subservient dedication of oneself to the rule of transcendent Reason, has been largely replaced by a new rationalism that is concerned rather and only with the appropriateness of instrumental means to unscrutinized ends. Classically, Europe had held that to seek what is not morally good is as irrational as to think what is not intellectually true.

Secularism in this new sense, then, has become an ideology that holds that there is nothing higher in the universe than we. Many of its victims have not only believed this, but have even felt it. Some, to the devastation also of their neighbours, have even begun to live in terms of it. In a milder version, even if one feels that there is more to human life and to the world than objectively appears, yet one is not allowed to think it. Especially, one is not allowed to think it publicly. Most people do feel it, except that growing number of the alienated and despairing, for whom the world and especially their own lives are bleak.

This brings us to the secular-religion polarity. As remarked, 'secularism' began as anti-religious, tacitly meaning anti-Christian and anti-Jewish. Thus we come to the 'religious' issue in our topic. Let us note first of all that it was the rise of the secular movement in the West that led to the development of the concept of a 'religion' and of the adjective 'religious'. 'Religion' as the name of a particular system of ideas, practices, outlooks and institutions was not merely a Western term, and a recent one, but also a secularist one. The notion of secularism inherently presupposes something called 'religion' from which it advocates that we should be free. If there were no religion, there would and could be no concept 'secularism'. Similarly, however, though this fact has been less clearly noticed, if there were no secularism there would be and could be no concept 'religion'. The term 'religion' was developed by secularists in order to belittle it.

'Religion' is a secular concept.

Before we expand that point, let us first note that the growth of the awareness of a diversity of our planet's civilizations and cultures and ideologies enlarged secularism's disparagement of religious movements but did not substantially change it. Christians and Jews had suffered from an exclusivist theology which not merely failed to appreciate alternative forms of spirituality to their own but came out as a positive decrying of them. Secularists were happy to join in this. They and Christians were at loggerheads at home, but co-operated in jointly disparaging abroad all human cultures' inherent propensity to recognize what I am calling the transcendent dimension of our life and of the world, and to express this culturally. Thus the secularists lumped together all the spiritual traditions of our planet beyond the West's borders under their heading of 'religions', despite the stark differences among them.

They ran into some trouble in certain cases, however, for there were instances where spiritual traditions of the rest of the world resembled the one spiritual tradition of the West, that from Greece & Rome, as much as or more than it did the other, that from Palestine. One example is Indian philosophy, which was recognizably comparable to Greek metaphysics but also could hardly help but be recognized as religious at the same time. Another difficulty came with the Ju chiao in China, which the West perhaps misleadingly dubbed 'Confucianism': it has never been quite able to decide whether this should be classed as 'a religion' or as 'a philosophy', as if everything on earth could and should be forced into this specific pair of Western categories. The secularists preferred 'philosophy', because they felt an affinity for Confucian thought and did not wish to be caught liking a religion. Religious people also felt an affinity; and they felt that by thinking of it as a philosophy they would not be precluded from that feeling of affinity by their Western rule of not more than one 'religion' at a time. For a while there was difficulty also in the West's deciding whether Shinto is a religion. It was in the 19th century, I understand, that people in Japan coined a term to render in Japanese the Western import concept 'religion', but I am not sure whether they have found it helpful. It is interesting that the West, since propounding this concept, has never been able to define it. Everyone seems to know what it means, until they start thinking about it carefully.

On one point, however, in regard to the matter all secularists were agreed. This is their view of other people, and is a point that I wish to consider rather fully. We have remarked that exponents of any world-view categorize alternatives as abnormal. Every significant world-view works out ways of interpreting what they see around them in terms of their own conceptions. At first Western secularists had to deal only with the Christian fact, and to a minor extent the Jewish. Presently, however, as they themselves were becoming more detranscendentalized, they further discovered that virtually all the rest of humankind, far beyond the bounds of Christendom, were aware of transcendence, in one form or another, and took it seriously; were, as they put it, 'religious'—alas. They had early on, in their 'rationalist' zest, dismissed Christian and Jewish 'religion' as a great intellectual error; but with the rise of awareness of Asia, Africa, the islands, and all, they were forced to recognize two problems. First, if religion be intellectual error, there were a great many different ones—starkly different. Even the central error, as they saw it, of believing in God turned out not to cover all [so-called] 'religious' outlooks. Secondly, they were gradually forced to recognize that there is much more to the whole affair than the intellectual. They had developed the new notion of 'believing', as their view of what religious people basically do—a fallacy that I have recently been discovering, and demonstrating, to be both recent and profoundly misleading.[2] It is amazing, the extent to which we in the West have been manoeuvred into thinking about religion in secularist terms.

Although no one could define religion, they made attempt after attempt to explain it. Given that the huge majority of humanity turns out to be, and throughout to have been, 'religious', and given the growingly manifest fallacy of their predictions that, with modern progress, this would soon pass, the matter seemed more urgent; and there has actually been a shift recently from trying to explain religion—meaning, in effect, to explain it away—towards trying, more humbly, to understand it. A wide variety of sociological, psychological, and other explanations were put forward. Many of them were markedly illuminating, perhaps not of religion so much as of human nature. None was fully convincing, though several have been helpful. The explanations differed from each other, often deeply; indeed, several were mutually incompatible. Yet however much they differed on religion, all secularists agreed on one thing. And it is surprising how widespread this particular view has become, even beyond straight secularist circles.

That point of agreement is their postulate that human nature is fundamentally secular, and that religion is some sort of addendum. 'Religion' is something that some people 'have'. The secularist's problem then is to explain or to understand why we have it; or to persuade us to give it up. It is thought of as something that has as it were been tacked on here or there to a culture or a group or a person for one reason or another. The religions being seen as basically a series of misreadings of the world, each could, it is thought, be dropped without fundamentally changing our relation to each other or to the world or to ourselves—except perhaps for the better.

My central thesis is that this postulate, of religion as an addendum, can now be seen to be, simply, false. It is an ingredient in a particular ideology: necessary perhaps to sustain those who subscribe to that ideology, by justifying their particular outlook on the world; but it does not make sense of other outlooks, it cannot be applied to other cultures, either in the past or the present— nor, I am suggesting, in the future; and it cannot be used to interpret the entire world, or humanity as such.

The panorama of the world's cultural history recognizes that this particular secularist error is, in one sense, of a quite standard type. Each major human world-view has tended, especially in the West, to categorize alternatives as abnormal. It has satisfactorily interpreted to itself both the natural world that it knows, and its own vision. That is what a world-view is. Yet each has regularly failed to come up with an interpretation of other people's alternative world-views that does justice to those alternatives. Jewish, Christian, and Islamic understanding of non-Jewish, non-Christian, non-Islamic peoples has been strikingly inapt. Every outlook interprets in its own terms—of course—the rest of the world; but when one comes to know the rest of the world, which only nowadays are we in process of seriously doing on a large scale, one always finds that that particular outlook was indeed particular, was one among the others. All of us are challenged to modify the particularisms that we have inherited, in the direction of a universalism that will make sense in modern times.

This challenge has begun to be recognized by some of the major so-called religious movements, and serious efforts are being made by some among them to come to grips with the new pluralism. Those efforts may not be adequate to the crisis that pluralism poses, and one cannot be sure whether the rest of this century will perhaps be one of dreadful religious conflict. At least equally likely, alas, is the prospect of conflict involving ideologies, or between a so-called religious group and a secular group (as perhaps in the United States). Whatever the practical developments, we are concerned here with theory. My contention is that the secularist movement has not yet even begun to come to terms with pluralism, recognizing that secularism is not the 'normal' or given human condition, but is a new ideological movement that for good or ill has arisen (for good and ill, I would say: it has had many beneficial consequences, and many harmful ones, like most great human movements); and that it is one among others. Just as it was arrogant for Christians to assert that they are right and outsiders are misguided heathen, bifurcating humankind into the saved and the damned, so it is arrogant for secularists to have divided humankind into secular and religious.

There is a classical Muslim saying that God creates every infant inherently *muslim*, but his parents make him a Christian or a Jew or a Zarathustrian. Precisely parallel is the secularist view that every child is, as it were, born inherently secular, is ideally secular, but their parents or their society or their failure to cope realistically with the world make them religious. Certainly they see religion as a deviation from the right and proper way, or anyway from the rational and true.

In rejecting as untenable the secularist postulate that what it calls religion is an addendum to the human condition, I am not saying that human nature is basically 'religious'. To say that would be to accept the dichotomy between secularism and religion. What I am saying is that that either/or dichotomy is not sound. By that,

I mean that it will not stand up to a modern awareness of the facts: neither of ourselves nor of other people; neither of past history nor of present—nor, I imagine, will it stand up to the future.

For one thing, adherents of all other positions than one's own do not constitute a single category, in essence undifferentiated. There is as much difference between certain forms of Hindu thought and Christian, or between Jewish and Buddhist, as there is between any of these and certain secularist positions. It is sloppy thinking to imagine that all so-called religious positions can be lumped together as of one sort, with the secularist as of a basically different sort.

My more basic objection, however, is of another type.

The fact is that for human beings, and doubly so for human communities, to be in one way or another what has come to be called 'religious' is altogether normal. It is inherently right and proper, the standard everyday human situation. It is what one would expect, if one understands what it means to be human. To think of it as odd or bizarre, as something extraneous, over and above the ordinary, is inapt.

I make these statements on the basis of the facts of world history. I am not suggesting that all 'religious' systems—I would say, all human systems—are wonderful or true. I do not think that they are. To affirm that the so-called religious is part of the human, is not to neglect the point that human beings can be, and have been, not only at times sublime in vision and admirable in constructive achievement individual and corporate, but also at other times grotesque, wicked, and silly, destructive of themselves and of others. Usually, we have been and have done between the extremes. In any case normally we have fallen short, whether little or woefully much, of even our limited ideals. Always our concepts, our activities, even our aspirations, have been those of finite beings.

Most of us have averred that indeed we are finite, but that we are not utterly cut off from some relation to the infinite, or at least to something higher than ourselves. To be human means to live in an environment that includes the world of things; includes each other—and our relations with each other are among the most central aspects of ourselves—and includes a realm loftier than ourselves in our empirical actuality. So most persons, most societies, most centuries, have reported. I am suggesting that in this they have been right. There in fact is such a third order of reality, and humanity consistently has been and is aware of it, however dim or tentative the awareness may have been (sometimes accounts of it have not been tentative! Most have called it not a third order but the first, with the others derivative or otherwise subordinate). Whether it be continuous with the lower orders, or discrete, or overlapping, or virtually identical though diversely perceived, is a question to which diverse answers have been given; but that there is in fact something there, few have failed to recognize.

It is secularism, therefore, not something called religion, that needs to be explained; secularism in its recent nihilist version. It is the anomaly. I have already indicated that for a time secularism and humanism were simply among the many ways in which a movement has set forth in concepts its particular and finite aware-ness of transcendence, its specific selection of aspects of it that have caught that movement's attention and that it wishes to emphasize. More recently, however, its articulation intellectually of its particular vision has denied that that transcendence is there. This is unquestionably a human aberration. I contend that that is an intellectual error, and that it should be corrected.

It is an error on two counts, one of which it shares with many other major traditions, especially Western. Having intellectual errors it shares with all; or anyway with those that try to state their positions intellectually, in prose. Expressing in words and systematic concepts a full orientation to the universe is something constantly in need of revision, as new situations arise and new awareness becomes available; and the student of the history of religion notes that all major movements have in fact evinced con-stant dynamic, even though the form of the inherited vision is often felt to be so precious that a people is hesitant to tamper with it, so that change comes slowly—or is unacknowledged. Come it does, however; and come it must.

Until recently the Jewish and Christian, for instance, expressed their highly important sense of the meaning of human history partly through the idea that the world was created all of a sudden in 4004 B.C. It was a deeply painful and prolonged strug-gle that they went through to revise this mistake; but they have eventually largely done so. Again: to a large extent Christians, Jews, and the Islamic movement, have interpreted the universe in ways that have made sense of their own positions but have drastically failed to appreciate, and even to make room for, other peoples' spiritual life. Their understanding of fellow human beings at this point has involved a deeply serious intellectual error, with exceedingly serious practical consequences. To correct it is proving again painful, and apparently will be slow, but that must be done. Some of us who are Christians are working hard at this. This is the error that they and the secular movement share. It is part of Western arrogance: the 'we are right, the rest of you are wrong' attitude. Secularists' interpretation of their fellow human beings' positions, which because transcendentalist they dismiss, is comparably seriously mistaken, and will have to be revised.

In this case the damage done by the error has been grievous not only at the level of inter-community and inter-civilization harmony, with the consequent failure to play a constructive role in one of the world's decisive challenges to-day: that of building a pluralist planet of peace and concord. So dominant in political affairs has the secular outlook become that there is potentially disastrous failure to recognize how basic, how integrally important, are what they see as 'merely religious' concerns to political, social, and economic patterns throughout much of the world. The damage done by the secularist error has been equally or even more profound, however, within its own movement and within the societies where its view of things has risen to power. This is the second, related, count on which I spoke of its mistake.

The fact demonstrably is that human nature is inherently aware of, sensitive to, responsive to, what I am calling transcendence in its environment and within itself; and always has been so, the records indicate, since the dawn of human emergence on this planet. The awareness has taken an enormous variety of forms. A small number of them have become great world movements embracing many millions of persons and enduring over many centuries. One of the forms that it has taken in Western civilization has been the legacy from Greece & Rome, a form that is called secular. Other forms, in both East and West, have been called religions. Although these forms substantially differ among themselves, nonetheless an equally significant matter, both historically and personally, is the differing degree to which individual persons, various societies, and diverse eras have been aware, sensitive, responsive.

Islam, for example, is a great system, rich, noble, enormously impressive. It is not transcendent; though at its best it may orient its adherents to transcendence. More important than whether a given person is a Muslim or not—itself a mundane, not a transcendence-oriented, question—is how perceptive that person is, how sensitive, discerning, loyal, to the transcendence that the Islamic forms may make available. The Islamic tradition exists in this world, empirically, mundanely, observable to those of us on the outside. It exists as the result, however, of persons in the past having sensed to a certain degree and in a certain fashion the transcendent dimension to human life and to the world, and their having articulated that sense in certain forms; and it has continued to exist, carried forward and developed in succeeding generations, because through the forms of that tradition they also have been encouraged, and enabled, to some degree to sense those dimensions. How successful a given person, group, or century has been, however, in discerning it, how loyal to that discerning, how effectively each has lived out the discernment, has been a matter constantly at issue—and varying between extremely wide margins.

Some have been loyal to the forms and to the system more than to the transcendent reality for which those forms and that system might have served as a channel. Some have been destructive, fiercely devoted to Islam more than humbly to God, counting it a virtue to be mercilessly fanatical to the system rather than recognizing the virtue of mercy to which the system at its best points, and personalizing that mercy. Islam may be a religion; but in any case the transcendent transcends Islam. It is the business of the Islamic system to serve it, and this it may do well or badly, variously from time to time, from place to place, from group or person to group or person.

The same may be said of Christianity, Buddhism, or the rest. Each is interesting. The most interesting question, however, is not about each tradition as objects, but about people, and about centuries. Do these, or do they not—more accurately, to what extent and in what directions do they—sense the transcendent reality in which our lives are embedded, and act in terms of that sense?

The secular tradition in the West, I have argued, was another such form. The ideas and ideals of Greek philosophy, the aesthetic forms of classical poetry and rhetoric and art, the humanist ideal, the rationalist vision, the dream of a good social order, all arose because some persons were indeed perceptive of a truth, a beauty, a justice of which they caught a powerful glimpse, and indeed were able to give form to their vision, in ideas and patterns that could and did then serve others for many generations. Some who inherited this tradition were more, some less, responsive through those forms to the transcendent reality that these in part enshrined.

Each tradition, being finite, has even at its best drawn attention to some facets only of the transcendence to which humanity is open. This is apart from the fact that each participant in that tradition has him- or herself grown to varying degrees actively or even passively aware of certain aspects of those various facets.

Of every great tradition the adherents are in danger of losing sight of the transcendence to which its purpose was to point. Also, every tradition, by articulating its vision in specific forms, is in danger of limiting the limitless. Western secularists began to do that limiting when instead of supplementing the Christian vision, or modifying it, they started to deny it. It has since moved into a stage where many of its former devotees have indeed lost sight of transcendence almost entirely. Some, as we have said, have even denied that it is there, and denied that an essential characteristic of human nature lies in our being open to it. This is in a sense ridiculous; but more important, it is tragic. It is foolish to suggest that human beings are unaware that truth is higher than falsehood, and is higher than we: we can catch hold of only a fraction of truth, and even that never absolutely, yet what we catch is precious. It is foolish to suggest that human beings are unaware that good is higher than bad; that integrity is better than dishonesty. It is foolish, and sad, not to recognize that an individual becomes a full person only in community. It is obtuse, and pathetic, not to sense the refreshment and uplift to the human spirit that can come to us through the beauty of the natural world. And so on. I mention only a few among the more immediate of the many matters that range on and on to the highest reaches to which humanity has shown itself at times sensitive.

Not only, however, is it foolish, this intellectual error. It has also begun to be devastating, socially and personally. Alas.

We remarked above that the universe is in motion. Spiritual movements too are dynamic, changing from generation to generation; and so are the intellectual accounts that they give of and for themselves. As an historian of religion and culture, I know very well that every tradition, religious and other, has been different every century from what it was the century before. We hope and strive that Christian theology, for instance, will correct its major errors, especially on the pluralist question. Let us hope and strive that the secular ideology do so also. I am not optimistic that all will be in conceptual order in time. Yet neither am I pessimistic. I do not know the future. I do have a sense as to our task in the present, to prepare for it.

Thus the point broached by my title arises, in this: That if secularism and humanism change their theories so as to make intellectual room within them for the valid existence in the world of what they call the 'religious' movements, and for the human recognition that there is more to the world, to each other, to ourselves, than meets the eye, then there will be no point any more in our calling all the other forms in which human beings express this recognition 'religious'. They will simply be known for what they are: varying attempts to be truly human, and to make sense of this not quite inscrutable universe in which we live. Human beings will continue to be Christian or Buddhist or Tenri or Muslim, or humanist in a transcendentalist sense, since such movements will forge ahead; just as we shall continue to be Canadian or Japanese, or black or brown, and male or female. All these matters are important; but are less ultimately important than the transcending matter that we all share. That includes the imperative, and rewarding, task of understanding.

Next century then will not be concerned with the question of being secular or religious. It will give its attention to the important matter, of how to live in this universe well, ourselves and in harmony with others—and how to learn about this from our inherited traditions, and from each other.

I myself, for instance, am a modified Christian. I am not, however, 'religious' in some odd sense; I am simply a normal human being who happens to be reasonably alert to what is going on in the world and in the universe. I participate—not uncritically; yet gratefully—in the ever-changing Christian movement, as my particular instance of world-wide, history-long, human alertness. I do not believe everything that the Church tells me; I have already remarked that believing is not a significant criterion of Christian or Islamic or Buddhist life. And I do not feel that everyone else ought to be Christian, any more than I feel that you Japanese ought to be Canadian, or that black or brown people ought to be yellow or white; or that women ought to be men or men women. I do feel that we all ought to learn from each other, and ought to learn how to get along well together in a crowded world. It has been my special privilege to have learned a great deal from Buddhists, Muslims, humanists, and many others; so that, for one thing, I know that it can be done, and is enriching. I realize that some Buddhists, for instance, have evidently seen some facets of the truth that I have not, or not yet, been able to see—I have tried, but there are some of their perceptions that I have not understood; and Christians, for example, have seen some that most Muslims have not yet been able to see—many have not tried. We have all learned from modern secularism, but also the rest of us have seen something that nihilistic secularists have yet to learn. If things go well, the 21st century will have made substantial progress towards sharing insights.

My argument in this presentation, you may have noticed, has not been secular rather than religious, nor religious rather than secular. It is itself not either/or. It has aspired to be based on empirical facts, as observed by historical study; to proceed by rational argument; and to contend that the goal is to discern and to live out the proper way to be fully human. It is because I am a secular humanist—but not in the nihilist or any negative sense—that I have come to recognize that we are, and the world is, in profound trouble unless we are also and deeply what my fellow secular humanists call religious.

CHAPTER 6

Islamic Resurgence

The interpretation of current developments in the Muslim world proffered in this paper endeavours to set them in historical context, even at times rather long-range. Also, it presents them in terms of involvement with the West. One might imagine that that is what would be expected of me, since I am an historian and a comparativist. Actually, however, it is the other way 'round. I gradually became an increasingly long-range historian after having begun to study current affairs in Muslim societies, and finding that my attempts to understand at a serious level what is now going on, first in the Arab world and more especially in India, and later in other cases, pushed me ever more deeply into a large historical approach; and finally also into a comparativist one. This last was because the development of any society proves on scrutiny to be inter-involved with that of neighbouring ones around the world: covertly so in the more distant past; more and more conspicuously, of course, in our century. By 'history' I mean not the past, as do some—and certainly not the study of the past, which is historiography, and is a present-day activity. Rather, to me history is a process: one that began no doubt long since, but continues to-day, with—the optimists among us hope—a future still to come, currently being fashioned. The most interesting chapter in Islamic history to date is the one currently being written by the Muslims, and/or being written for them by outsiders, but it is only one chapter following the fourteen centuries' that have gone before. It is not perhaps the greatest chapter: greatness lies for them, they feel, manifestly in the past; and, they dream, or resolve, also somewhere in the next fourteen.

I begin my presentation, then, with two historical incidents, separated from each other by a thousand years. The first is from Cordoba, in Muslim Spain, in the mid-10th century A.D.; the second, from the U.S. at the beginning of the last decade. I see certain parallels that can be drawn between the two.

The first scene, in Cordoba, took place when the world was going through a different phase from now. The incident that I proffer occurred at the rather splendid court of the Muslim caliph 'Abd al-Rahman III; the occasion is the formal visit to that court of Queen Toda of Navarre, along with her young grandson Sancho el Gordo. Before I mention the official objectives of her mission, and its substantial results, let us notice something of the setting. The surrounding scene was impressive. 'Abd al-Rahman was one of the wealthiest, most powerful, most cultured, and most able monarchs on this planet at that time. His court, and his situation, were grander than even his rival Muslim caliph's at Baghdad. The then Japanese capital at Kyoto might perhaps be compared— although the two courts were unaware of each other. Certainly there was nothing in Western Europe to compare. 'Abd al-Rahman himself had ruled long and had worked hard and well. His navy was without question the most powerful in the world. His domain was prospering and at peace. Queen Toda, whose realm of Navarre was one of the minor principalities to the north—in Christendom—, was greatly impressed by what she saw. The city itself, a much bigger metropolis than she had ever known, she found imposing. Surprisingly, the streets were paved, were lit at night by street lamps, there were several hundred public baths, many public libraries, hospitals, and schools, and of course splendid mosques. She admired the recently completed and sumptuous summer retreat nearby which the caliph had had erected with funds bequeathed to him by a wealthy concubine to ransom Muslim prisoners of war but it had been found that there were none of these.

Queen Toda's purpose was on behalf of her grandson, and was twofold. She had come to seek medical help: 'Sancho el Gordo' means 'Sancho the Fat', and evidently his obesity was indeed striking. Also, she had come to seek political help, towards realizing his claim to the throne of Navarre's neighbouring municipality, León. In due course her mission proved successful on both counts. Medically, the boy was treated by the caliph's prime minister, one Hasdai ben Shaprut, a Jewish physician. (Readers will recall that at this time in Western Europe—shall we not say, in Christendom—not many Jews were chief ministers, or held major public office!) And presently, in no insignificant part through this court's influence, her son did indeed become king of León.

An analogy with the present day, but in reverse, is I hope obvious. One knows of instances when in our day, from the under-developed countries (among which at that time Europe of course was), persons in a position to make the trip visit, say, New York for advanced medical treatment; and petty rulers or would-be rulers visit Washington in the hopes that the great power will, by pulling appropriate strings, help to actualize some desired local political goal back home; and in the course of their visit are deeply impressed by the sights that they observe.

The other occasion that I conjure up here is, as I said, a recent one—from the beginning of the last decade: the U.S./Iranian hostage issue. Americans called this 'the Tehran crisis'; I, who was living in the States at the time, came to think of it rather as the American crisis, into such stark turmoil emotionally was this country thrown by the events. U.S. society was deeply startled and disturbed; and when the group of Americans being held finally returned home, this nation was exuberant. One can learn something from this, I felt. Not irrelevant, surely, was that it followed on the tense confusion—shall we say, disaster—of Vietnam. My suggestion was that a nation recently grown accustomed to being great, powerful, accustomed to the feeling of getting what it wanted if it tried hard, was both bewildered and furious to find itself being pushed around by what it irritatedly called a 'little pip-squeak' group of 'nasty foreigners', and to find itself apparently impotent. Americans do not like being pushed around.

Neither do Muslims. I have related my tale of Cordoba to remind us that for several centuries the Islamic world was an unchallenged great power, and centre of culture and sophistication. It was Muslims who wrote the letters of credit, as well as the poetry; who were world leaders not only in banking and navy dominance but in mathematics and science, in historiography and architecture; of whom other people were at times afraid, or whom others envied or emulated, while Muslims themselves lived in prosperity and enormous and well grounded self-confidence. As is well known, the first period of the brilliant success of Islamic civilization was presently dealt a severe blow with the fall of Baghdad to the Mongols in the 13th century, and of Spain to the Reconquista in the 15th. Yet that civilization presently not only recovered but resumed its triumphant onward march. This is represented in the

16th and 17th centuries by the Ottoman, the Persian, and the Indian Muslim empires, all magnificent; and by the expansion of the Islamic community by conversion into much of Africa, Indonesia, and to a less extent elsewhere, such as China.

By the 18th century, on the other hand, this world greatness of the Islamic movement had begun to peter out, just as the West was blossoming and expanding in the greatest outburst of energy that the world had ever seen. Presently most Muslim countries were, simply, conquered by the West. All were soon economically and to some degree culturally dominated.

It is not pleasant, after being dominant, to feel oneself debased, and demeaned. However true may be the poet's dictum that it is better to have loved and lost than never to have loved, some Canadians, for instance, maybe self-righteously feel that it is better—simpler, anyway—never to have had great power than to have had it and lost it. The election of Reagan, the seizure of Grenada (my father's original home, it so happens), the obsessive arms build-up in the 80's, were in part moves of an American populace resolute to gain back that power, and not to let it be jeopardized again. As I have said, Americans do not like being pushed around.

As I have also said, neither do Muslims. A good deal of their current mood is a resolve to throw out the alien civilization that has humiliated them; to re-assert their own; and to regain the power that they have lost.

One might almost imagine—if I may be allowed a fanciful flight of conjecture—that Americans since Vietnam and the hostage crisis should of all people be the ones most able to understand the plight and mood of Muslims, recognizing that they too have been smarting under a great reversal of fortune. The United States, after all, has been top dog for only a few decades, and has suffered only minor set-backs, compared to the centuries of Islamic pride and then the radical subjection to outsiders. Muslims had a century or two to brood over their loss of power and prestige; and to feel that they were paying for it dearly.

All this sets the stage for the modern situation; but not yet for the current one. There intervened a period of half a century or more, when the encounter with the West was fruitful. We might call it the liberal period; better, the Western-liberal period. For some Muslims it began, of course, earlier; and for some continued later, and indeed still continues. In general, however, we may say that this phase of Islamic history began on a substantial scale near the beginning of this century, and has of late shown signs of being superseded by a newer phase, of what I am calling 'Islamic resurgence'.

From the point of view of many of those participating in this newer movement, as well as from that of various Western observers who may deplore it, the chief explanation for the rise of the newer venture is what is perceived as the failure of the immediately preceding one. Some would say, the abject failure. The resurgence of what may be called conservative or traditional Islam (either adjective over-simplifies) is a result of the community's having tried for a couple of generations or so to fashion itself in terms of a Westernizing liberalism, and finding that it has not worked. That the experiment failed is a moral judgement on the part of Muslims turning from it to the other. On the part of neutral outside observers it is an historical judgement: one based on at least its evident failure to win the support of the newer generation, and of groups that now seem increasingly numerous. There are other grounds for the historical judgement, also, which I will endeavour to set forth and to elucidate.

To illustrate the broad movement and to epitomize the liberal failure, I once again select two single episodes as illuminating. First is the role of the late Shah of Iran. In short compass his career poignantly sums up embarrassingly much of the whole matter. He was educated at the University of California, and after graduating returned to his own country brimming with Western secular liberalism, an intelligent and emancipated free-wheeling chap, vaguely idealist. He set about to effect what both he and his fellow-travellers, and the Western world, all called the 'modernizing' of his country. (We have tended to hold that modernization is the process of becoming like us.) The veiling of women (as it was called; no one at that point spoke of women's veiling of themselves) was made illegal; large-scale land reform was pushed; revenues from the world oil market flowed in; motor cars and television sets became common in Tehran, and jazz music and night clubs: affluence and alcohol.

Lord Acton long ago summed up his observation of human history in one generalization, 'Power corrupts, and absolute power corrupts absolutely'; and the maxim was not to be cheated in this instance. The Shah gradually developed from being a young modernizing idealist into a not so young and, we now realize, brutal dictator. The good times of those who prospered rested increasingly on a ruthless oppression and terrorizing of the rest.

Decisive in all this was a close collaboration maintained with the West, especially America. The Shah sided with the United States, and the West generally, in social and personal outlook and economic policy, and received much help, especially in building up ('modernizing') his army. (Oil meant wealth and cosmopolitanism for him and Iran; it meant strategic importance for Washington, which also had years before paved the way for his reign by using the C.I.A. to overthrow Iran's less Westernizing reformer Musaddiq ['Musaddegh'].) Washington also, Iranians soon discovered, helped train the Shah's secret police to torture and mutilate them when they showed discontent.

The tragedy of modern Iran is of course not altogether the West's fault, centrally incriminated although we unquestionably are. Without Western involvement it would not have happened (more on this later); yet neither would it have happened were it not that the Shah became an immoral man. The morale of a society, and the day-to-day moral stature of its members, are historically consequential matters. My thesis is that in this case the lack of moral character of the Shah was neither fortuitous nor altogether atypical. Liberal values and ideas, like any others, are effete and in the end vacuous without persons' faith in them, which means interiorized commitment to them, stamina in pursuing them, seeing and feeling them as having priority over one's individual 'self-interest'. The ability to get up early in the morning, to work hard, to turn down bribes, to respect other people, to know and to feel that the general good is more important than private gain, is just as important in building and holding a liberal society as it is for any other. In Muslim countries, the only basis for morality and morale is—has been—Islam. (To this point too we shall return.) The Shah was more powerful than most, and more wicked than most; but throughout the Muslim world Westernized liberals as a class have repeatedly demonstrated an inadequate firmness in their loyalty to liberalism. This is normally not their own fault so much as it is due to an inadequate cultural underpinning for that loyalty. Western liberalism has largely been an alien value-system without foundations in Muslims' lives on which it can rest and by which it can be nourished and transmitted.

Again, however, the role of the West here has been crucial. My second illustrative scene is from Beirut in the early 1950's. I was chatting with a delightful, intelligent, cultured, generous Arab intellectual with a degree from the Sorbonne, who told me of his dispiritedness over the way things were going. 'I broke from my family tradition,' he told me, 'from my religion, from my culture, and cast in my lot with the new vision of the West. Relatives and friends accused me of betraying my people and its past; but I held firm to my new loyalties, and have lived and thought as a cosmopolitan in comradeship with the modern West. And now the West has utterly let us down. Virtually all the West's liberals have sided with Zionism against us.' He was not complaining, so much as asking me if I could explain why liberals in Europe and America, priding themselves on fairness and justice and compassion for the uprooted, also for their commitment to the rights of peoples to freedom in their national homelands, showed so little sympathy for, or interest in, Arabs dispossessed of a land that had been theirs for long over a thousand years; and indeed so little concern or fellow-feeling for either Arabs or Muslims, so little appreciation of the religion and culture of Islam. At the time I realized only very partially how trenchant his question was and especially was going to be; or how widespread and significant the feeling would become that for a Muslim to think of the West, even of its liberal movement, as a friend is to be doomed to bitter disillusionment.

Zionism, and the Western support for Zionism, have come to crystallize a profound sense throughout the Muslim world that the West is not merely indifferent but fundamentally hostile to Muslims; and that even the West's liberal wing will in a crisis turn against them.

Recent deliberate deception of Muslim nations by the 'Christian' or liberal West will be doing little to dispel this deep (and sorrowful) sense that we do not see them as equals or treat them with serious respect. The Gulf War, more recently, with its dropping of 80,000 tonnes of bombs on Iraq, carried to new heights Western hostility to Islam and the Muslim world. And nowadays we cannot but be struck—those of us who notice it, that is—by the outpouring of both sympathy and support for the people of Haiti in their effort to overthrow a military government that suppressed a democratic election, simultaneous with the West's manifest sympathy and support of, rather, the military government in the remarkably parallel case of Algeria when there too a military régime suppressed a democratic election. The contrast is obviously on the grounds that the populace in *that* case is Muslim and was voting for an Islamic order.

I have long argued that indeed an underlying enmity of the West for Islam has been of major significance, especially since lately it has been largely unconscious, yet unrelenting. This again is an historical point, of the long-range sort. Few Westerners have any inkling of how their perceptions of Islam follow a pattern set by the Crusades and in general by fourteen centuries of animosity and, for long, fear. Of Hindu and Buddhist cultures—India, China, Japan— the West became aware only recently, after having become powerful and grandly self-confident and after it could loftily afford to be at times patronizing. Of Islam, on the other hand, it has throughout been sharply aware, the two having shared a common frontier from the start, in the 7th century. For a millennium the two civilizations met, often on battlefields, with the West repeatedly suffering defeat (except for the Crusades, an aggressive, but temporary, interruption). Until the rise of Marxism, Islam was the only world movement of which the West has been afraid. Spiritually, also: Islam is the only religious movement in the world that attracted many converts away from the Christian form of faith and from the Christian community (by the millions). In the Middle Ages, a widespread Western perception of Islam was of something Satanic. Muhammad was pictured as a fiend with horns. Europe was frankly scared. And fear generated hatred. Even to-day, lesser distortions are constant in the media, of a kind that would be quite libellous under anti-defamation rubrics if perpetrated against other groups. People who have no idea that they are involved in these bitter legacies from a distant past prolong or are victims of a scurrilous denigration of Muslims and Islam.

We are involved here in a new and ugly form of anti-Semitism. (The Arabs are also Semites.)

The long-standing enmity between the West and Islam, Islam and the West, works of course both ways. Only for a few centuries have Muslims been seriously afraid of the West; but current hostility has long historical roots to draw on. We have been their traditional enemy, as they have been ours, alas.

Western liberals, especially intellectuals, proud of their secularism, resist the charge of being caught up in these out-of-date religious considerations. In fact the early heritage still colours perceptions unwittingly. Yet in any case secularism has problems of its own. Western civilization is dual, one part of its inheritance coming from Greece and Rome, the other from Palestine. The two have proceeded sometimes in conflict, sometimes in harmony, sometimes juxtaposed, but never fused. In recent centuries, Western secularism, sufficiently dominant of late to be unselfconscious, has developed the concept 'religion' to designate the other of these two traditions—and to designate also other movements around the world which it has named 'Hinduism', 'Buddhism', and the like, and Islam. Western secularists are profoundly convinced that religion either is a fallacy from the past, or else in any case is something to be distinguished from the rest of culture and separated from most of it, and especially from politics, law, and economics. Islam, however, is not a religion in this sense. Islamic civilization has been unitary, not dual. One misunderstands Islam if one fails to see it as the counterpart both of the West's Graeco-Roman tradition and of its Palestinian. I said earlier that Westernizing liberals in the Islamic world lacked a moral foundation for their liberalism. Secular Western liberals often forget how fundamental for theirs has been the West's classical tradition, with its further development at the Renaissance and the Enlightenment: a tradition that in world-historical perspective must be seen as one of our planet's great spiritual heritages, with its metaphysical rationalism, its concept of justice, and especially with its humanism as a particularly major force. (This tradition has had not only its intellectual expositors but also its art, its music, its institutions, and its martyrs.) When early this century the great Turkish intellectual Ziya Gökalp advocated that Turkey become a secular state, the concept 'secular' was first rendered as *la-dini*, 'non-religious'; but in Turkish this adjective popularly meant 'dishonest', 'immoral', and it seemed bizarre to be clamorously advocating an immoral government system. The solution found was to coin then a new term in Turkish, *laik*, imported from the French *laique*. Leading Turks made an heroic endeavour to import the vision as well as the word; but that sort of transplant is precarious.

The Western failure to understand that (and why) Muslims cannot shunt 'religion' aside and have anything of significance or worth left, has bedevilled much of Western foreign policy, aid policy, and intellectual discourse. There was for at least fifty years, I believe, a major possibility of the next phase of Islamic history being liberal; but it would have been, would have had to be, an Islamic liberalism, a liberal Islam. There are certainly elements in the Muslim tradition on which that could be constructed, and therefore rendered effectively operative in Muslim society. Western liberalism, however, and even to a considerable extent then its Muslim converts, took an emphatically different line. It held, well-meaningly but ineptly, that progress, in a liberal sense (was any other imagined?), was an alternative to Islam, or at best was something parallel with it. Islam, as merely a religion, was seen as something that in these matters did not, and should not, count. I am endeavouring to explain, it will be recalled, the failure of liberalism in the Islamic world. It is ironic that the above Western outlook has proven a sort of self-confirming prophecy. The rise of a newer and anti-liberal Islam is being interpreted here as not a result of liberal failure but rather as corroborating the Western-liberal thesis that religion and politics do not mix. Rather, one should say that in the Islamic case they cannot be separated; so that if they are not mixed well, they will be mixed badly.

Liberalism in the Muslim world must be an Islamic liberalism—or it will always fail.

Another way of putting this point would be the following. In the 19th century, Christian missionaries from the West began with great confidence but ended by failing on the whole to convert Islam. In the 20th century the Western missionaries of secularism began with equal confidence, proved perhaps somewhat less unsuccessful, but they also are ending by failing on the whole to convert Islam. It has generated a deep crisis in Christian theology to have to come to a recognition that there are other religious visions as well as the Christian that must be comprehended in a global theory, of either the universe or human life. Secularist intellectuals have hardly begun as yet to wrestle with the fact that secularism too is one human vision among others, is an ideology of dignity and worth but not necessarily the best, and its categories certainly are not universally applicable (are not straightforwardly true).

This is not the place, however, to develop that large thesis. What is directly germane, for understanding the current Muslim scene, is the growing number of persons in the West who feel that liberalism has failed also here. That secularism has failed is the view underlying the rise of the so-called moral majority. Their disillusionment has led them to the sort of right-wing fundamentalism and religious reactionary stance that I myself certainly decry and imagine that many of my readers probably will too. That right-wing movement indicates, I contend, not that religion is inherently reactionary—I know too much history to be dupe of that fallacy. It shows rather that in the recent phase of Western history we liberals have failed to work out a general vision sufficiently moral and spiritual to be viable, and/or a religious vision sufficiently authentic and rich.

I certainly join in deploring a Falwell or a Khumayni. Yet even in the face of their movements, liberal secularists these days are in no position to feel self-righteous. After all, the substantially still more horrendous threat to each one of us and to humankind at large comes from secularism's proud progress in science, technology, and nationalism, with pollution of the oceans and the air and the earth, the accelerating arms race, and the stark possibility of nuclear winter. Liberalism in the West was a mighty movement of the human spirit, comparable in world-history perspective to other great spiritual and religious movements that have arisen and flourished. And my heart is in large part still very much with it. Yet must we not recognize that it has flourished less long than have several others, is proving inadequate sooner and at least as seriously as they. Many voices would say, 'even more inadequate'; would say that alas it is manifestly now turning sour.

Whatever be one's personal judgement on these issues, two facts stand out in elucidating the apparent failure of liberalism in the contemporary Islamic world. Muslims eager to prove that the promising future of that world lies with a return to Islam rather than with a merging with the liberal West, point to two hard-to-confute present-day realities. One is the apparent moral and social decline of the West, from overt matters strident to outsiders, such as family breakdown, pornography, rape, the upsurge in crime and violence, to more subtle developments such as the blatant insincerity of advertising, aggressive competition, the focus on means rather than ends, and the forlorn loneliness of modern-Western life. And of course behind it all looms the madness of nuclear war—receded for the moment, apparently, but not yet exorcised.

The other fact to which Muslim critics of the West point is that Westerners themselves are fast becoming disillusioned with our current scene. A number of leading Western thinkers are critics of the culture, often severe critics. The status quo, nowadays the *fluxus quo*, comes in for considerable assault. It is possible to interpret this Western self-criticism as a sign of vitality, freedom, and hope. One finds that interpretation in modern Arabic, Persian, Urdu, or Indonesian writing rarely, if at all. Rather, the self-criticism is cited regularly with the implied or stated commentary: 'Look, it is absurd of us Muslims to hitch our wagon to a star that even its devotees are recognizing as setting'.

The West, in Muslim eyes, is losing or has lost its soul. And not all Westerners disagree. (It sometimes goes unnoticed in the West, by the way, that most Westerners long since traded in their soul for a self, a considerably more individualist and mundane, indeed isolated and self-centred, concept; and in recent decades even that seems to be giving way to an identity, rather—except that no one seems to have an identity: it would appear to be something that we are all supposedly in search of.)

I close by entering a couple of substantial caveats. In order to present a thesis, I have allowed myself no doubt to over-state it. Current developments in the Muslim world are complex. What we are calling Islamic resurgence is only one among them. Furthermore, for it I have pointed to some relevant considerations, not to all, hoping that these would help at least towards making it less unintelligible. After all, one cannot in a few pages capture a huge population involved in an intricately dynamic congeries of movements. The situation is not black-and-white: it is human.

Another perception worth our noting and placing alongside the suggestions already proffered is the following. There is in Europe to-day what could perhaps by stretching be called fancifully a sort of shadow cabinet of Muslim intellectuals and leaders in exile from their respective countries. It comprises ex-cabinet-ministers from Afghanistan and elsewhere, as well as ex-editors and ex-university professors and writers, who speak French and German and English as well as Arabic or Persian or Urdu or whatever, and who are thinking hard about contemporary things in the Muslim world and about a new day yet to come for which they plan and even are organizing. Some of them speak of the current 'rise of fascism' in the Muslim world. That phrase I find highly interesting, worth our pondering. The categories in terms of which one thinks are crucial. Most Westerners opt for words like 'Islamic fundamentalism' for present-day trends. These signify a particular sort of adverse judgement: of something religious in a narrow sense, something obscurantist, benighted; also, remote from us. To speak, on the other hand, of 'fascism', while no less deprecatory and indeed even more negative, modifies the perspective considerably. After all, fascism was something that *we* did, we in the West. Germany, it is often remarked, was in some ways the most cultured country in Europe, secular and enlightened. (It was also, I may add, reverting to my opening points, a country that had just suffered a defeat.) Fascism in the Muslim world understandably takes an Islamic form, just as in the West it takes a nationalist one, or in Stalinist Russia a communist one. Yet for some it could be quite salutary to see present-day right-wing Muslim movements as a modern aberration—with emphasis both on 'modern' and on aberrant. What these Westerners see and do not like may be discerned as not old-fashioned Islam unredeemed by Western wisdom ('the kind of thing one would expect from Muslims!'), but rather as a distortion of Islam reminiscent of Western distortions.

My own title, also, 'Islamic Resurgence', may be an unhappy choice (although it is better than 'resurgence of Islam'—which sees Islam as a noun, a thing; we do better to think of it as adjectival, to think in terms of people, ones who are Muslim). I have not endeavoured to analyse what it purports to name, readers will have noticed; only to suggest some reasons for its rise. I myself do not adopt the term 'fascism'; we do not know yet whether the closer analogy even in those special areas where that might apply may not be rather to the excesses of the Terror that was the price paid for the French Revolution. Nor do we know yet whether an analogy may prove not too ridiculous to the Protestant Reformation, which also began by presenting itself as a conservative movement returning to the original and the pure, whose emergence too was accompanied by much conflict and bloodshed, but which turned out in succeeding centuries to have been deeply and widely innovative, associated with novel developments in religious life, and in political and economic and linguistic and cultural.

Developments in the modern Muslim world are complex, and major. I can see dimly some facets of reasons for their emerging, perhaps; but do not feel that any of us can know how they will work out. This much we all know: that the Muslims involved in these matters are fellow human beings with whom we share the planet, like us in many ways, unlike us in some; and whom it is fascinating, and important, that we come to understand, and with whom it is requisite that we collaborate to build to-morrow's world.

CHAPTER 7

A Human View of Truth

In this paper I wish to present a position on the notion 'truth'; to develop it; and to argue on its behalf.

Let me begin with a statement of the thesis in highly summary form. Briefly, my suggestion is that the locus of truth is persons. Or, if not 'the' locus, at least a central locus: of considerably greater importance and primacy than is now usually recognized. Truth and falsity are often felt in modern times to be properties or functions of statements or propositions; my present proposal is that much is to be gained by seeing them rather—or at least by seeing them also, and primarily—as properties or functions of persons. It is not statements that are true or false but the use of them by individuals.

This then is in brief the position that I must now try to develop. To elucidate it I turn to Islamic civilization, to draw from it my illustrative material. I do so partly because that is the sector of human affairs that I have studied most closely. I do it also, in part, because I hold—I have found—that on principle there is illumination, and potential profit, in considering any human problem thus from an unwonted angle, and in a wider context; pondering how a matter has appeared to people in other civilizations, and comparing that with how it appears to us. A comparativist approach to almost any issue can prove not only refreshing but instructive: our civilization is no longer faring so gratifyingly that we can blandly ignore criteria that transcend it. Thirdly, this approach illustrates my thesis not only substantially but formally; it is part of my contention that academic study, in so far as it is a pursuit of truth, involves also the question of its truth for us, a question such as I here raise. Chiefly, however, I present this Islamic material because it seems to me saliently helpful: to illustrate with clarity and force a matter of significance for us all.

Naturally, I have no wish to involve more than is necessary those unfamiliar with Islamics in exotic technicalities. I can, I believe, make my point clear by calling attention simply to three roots in the Arabic language, around which Muslims crystallized their concepts on this central issue. These three will, I think, suffice to illumine for us the Islamic stance, and to set the stage for our consideration not only of their orientations but also then of our own.

The three Arabic terms are *ḥaqqa, ṣadaqa,* and *ṣaḥḥa.* All three have something to do with truth. Yet the three are quite distinct (and this fact in itself is instructive). If I might oversimplify in order to introduce my point, I would suggest that the first has to do with the truth of things, the second with the truth of persons, and the third with the truth of statements. But let me elaborate.

First, *ḥaqqa.* When I first learned Arabic, I was taught that *ḥaqq* sometimes means 'true', sometimes means 'real'.

Now this same remark, actually, had been made to me also about the Latin term *verus,* which can mean real, genuine, authentic, and also true, valid. When I came to learn Sanskrit, I met the same point again with regard to that language's (and civilization's) term *satyam*: it too denotes both reality, and truth. Eventually I came to realize that what was happening here was not necessarily that these peoples were somehow odd folk who had confused or converged two concepts, or used one word indiscriminately for two different notions; that perhaps it is we who are odd, are off the track, we who have somehow dichotomized a single truth-reality, and have allowed our concept of truth to diverge from our concept of reality.

But even in the West to-day we harbour remnants of this earlier usage. For our own civilization, decidedly, was built on concepts of this type. We still at times can speak of true courage, or false modesty; of true marriage or a true university; even of a true note in music. I mentioned this once, however, to a philosopher only to have him dismiss it as metaphorical, and not really legitimate or even significant. Only propositions, he said, are *really* true or false. And even the non-analysts among us, whatever our residual vocabulary, have come to feel a certain discomfort with any but a very imprecise position that things, qualities, actions, can be true or false. Things are just there, somehow, many feel, and it is only what we say about them that is subject to this discriminating judgement.

However that may be, in Arabic *ḥaqq*, like *satyam* and *veritas*, refers to what is real, genuine, authentic, what is true in and of itself by dint of metaphysical or cosmic status. It is a term supremely applicable to God. In fact, it refers absolutely to Him; *al-Ḥaqq* is a name of God not merely as an attribute but as a denotation. *Huwa al-Ḥaqq*: He is reality as such. Yet every other thing that is genuine is also *ḥaqq*—and, some of the mystics went on to say, is therefore divine. Yet the word means reality first, and then God, for those who equate Him with reality. (In passing, it is interesting to note that this in a sense makes it more engaging—perhaps more realistic—to talk about atheism in Arabic than in English, since in Arabic it can be a question of not believing in Reality, trusting in Reality, committing oneself to Reality, and the like. Yet I let that pass, simply noting that *ḥaqq* is truth in the sense of the real, with or without a capital R.)

Secondly, let us turn to the Arabic *ṣadaqa*. As I have remarked, this term refers to a truth of persons. It matches to some extent our Western notions of honesty, integrity, and trustworthiness; yet it goes beyond them. It involves being true both to oneself and to other persons, and to the situation with which one is dealing. Propositional truth is by no means irrelevant here. It is not ruled out; nor even set aside. Rather, it is subordinated, being incorporated as an element within a personalist context. For indeed the term is used predominantly, although not exclusively, for what we call 'telling the truth'. This is often the simplest way to translate it; yet there is something more. What that something more involves, at the personalist level, becomes apparent when we consider, in both Arabic and English, the contrasting concept of telling a lie. *Ṣadaqa* is the precise opposite of *kadhiba*, 'to be a liar'. In both Arabic and English this is a highly revealing usage: it denotes not only the saying of something that is untrue, but that the speaker knows it to be untrue and says it with an intent to deceive. The Arabs do not use *kadhiba*, as we do not use 'liar', when someone says something inaccurate but in good faith.

It is curious, as we shall develop later, that in English we have the concepts of 'lie' and 'liar' which correspond more or less exactly to the Islamic concept of *kadhiba*—a personal falsity, untruth at the level of human intent and practice, and of interpersonal relations—but we do not have an exact equivalent to, have not formulated a special concept for, the related concept of *ṣidq*: truth with a strictly personalist focus. (*Ṣidq* is the generic of *ṣadaqa*: what modern Westerners call the abstract noun, although for Arabs it is more strictly the verbal noun, the name of the action.)

This concept, then, has been a central one for Muslims, not least in their religious life, and is central too for the thesis that I am endeavouring to advance in this paper. I will return to pursue it further when I have dealt with the third term, *ṣaḥḥa*.

This verb, and its adjective *ṣaḥīḥ*, although expressing important concepts, have been less spectacular in Islamic life, and especially in the realm that concerns us here. The words mean, more or less, 'sound', and refer to quite a variety of matters, such as being healthy or being appropriate. One would hardly think of it as a term for 'truth' at all, except that it does, indeed, overlap in part with that English word in that it may be used in Arabic of propositions when they are what we would call true or correct. (*Hādhā ṣaḥīḥ, hādhā ghalaṭ*—or, *khāṭi'*; or simply *ghayr ṣaḥīḥ*.)

Of these three Arabic concepts, it is to be noted that the first two have strongly polarized contraries. *Ḥaqq* stands in stark and even awesome contrast to *bāṭil*, as the true and the false, or the real and the 'phoney'. Behind the one is metaphysical power, while the other, in strident dichotomy from it, is ludicrously vain and vacuous. To distinguish between the two is one of our most decisive tasks or prerogatives. Again, there is the resonant pair of *ṣidq* and *kadhib*, or to use the more concrete human terms, *ṣādiq* and *kādhib*: the honest person of truth stands sharply over against the despicable and wretched liar. At play here is the Islamic vision of our dramatic freedom and moral choice, in a world where decisions matter.

Ṣaḥīḥ, on the other hand, has no clear opposite. One of its applications is to a person's being in sound health; possible alternatives are that he or she may be weak, or sick, or old, or not old enough, or missing a limb, or what not; but there is no clear other pole. The only opposite of 'sound' is a wide range of unsoundness, of unspecified imperfections; although as we have already noted, in the particular case of a sentence, if it is not *ṣaḥīḥ*, true, then one may perhaps call it mistaken, *ghalaṭ* or *khāṭi'*. A railway timetable that is no longer in force, or an argument that is not cogent, various sorts of things that do not come off or are not in good working order, may be characterized as not *ṣaḥīḥ*; but this designates a quality that is not a category, or at least not a cosmic one. In other Islamic languages too—Persian, Urdu, and others, as well as Arabic—this third notion, used for, among other things, propositional truth, has by far the feeblest moral connotations of the three.[1]

Indeed, the first and the second are saturatedly, bristlingly, moral; they, and their respective pejorative contraries, are highly moralistic. Human destiny is at stake with them, and human quality. And, appropriately enough, it turns out on inquiry that the third root, *ṣaḥḥa*, does not even occur in the Qur'an. The other two reverberate in it, mightily.

It would hardly be an exaggeration to see the Qur'an as a vibrant affirmation that the *loci* of significant truth are two: the world around us, and persons. The reality of the former is divine, or is God. The inner integrity of the latter, and our conformity to, and commitment to, the real, are crucial. Indeed, this is what human life is all about.[2]

Let us return, however, to our specifically linguistic item: *ṣadaqa, ṣidq*. Being a resonant term in the Qur'an, it formulates for Muslims a cosmic category, constituting one of the basic points of reference in relation to which human life and society take on meaning. Even apart from the rest of that complex, however, I think that we may find it a strikingly interesting conceptualization in itself, one that will reward a rather careful unfolding.

First, let us look at the great medieval Arabic dictionaries, those marvellous mines of massive yet meticulous information. We find in them illuminating presentations and analyses of this word. Almost always these are given in conjunction with its correlative, *kadhiba*, 'lying'. The dictionary expositions in almost every case give first, or make quite basic, the link with speech. Yet even so it is (it and 'lying' are) applied to all sorts of things that we may say (and not only to what in modern logic would be called statements or propositions). Explicitly indicated is that the speech may be about the past or about the future, in the latter case whether by way of promise or otherwise; and may be indicative but also either interrogative or imperative, and even supplicative. Thus a question may be not *ṣidq*, truthful, if it involves something of the 'Have you stopped beating your wife?' sort. Similarly a command, such as

'Give me back my book', or an entreaty, 'Would you please give me back my book', may be *ṣidq* or *kadhib*, truthful or lying, depending upon whether the person addressed has the book, and the person speaking genuinely wishes it back.

In general, the dictionaries make it clear that the point is that *ṣidq* applies to that sort of speech in which there is conformity of what is said simultaneously with two things: (a) what is in the speaker's mind; and (b) what is actually the case.

Particular discussion is given to an assertion that 'Muhammad is the Apostle of God'—which is the Muslim's paradigm of a true statement—when it is made by someone who says it insincerely. One view is that any utterance may be half *ṣidq*, in reference either to the speaker's sincerity or to the objective facts, but there is full *ṣidq* only when both are satisfied. Similarly, when there is reference to the future, then *ṣidq* demands congruity both between inner conviction and the words spoken and between these latter and the subsequent deeds.

The verb may take as its direct object the person addressed, inasmuch as telling the truth, in this sense, and lying, are matters of personal interrelations. 'He lied to her', or 'P spoke the truth to Q', indicate that the truth and falsity under consideration here are attributes of a statement in its role of establishing or constituting communication between or among human beings. Here again, it may be noted that in the modern West we maintain in our conceptualization of lying the notion that one can hardly tell a lie alone on a desert island, but we have tended to let go of this interpersonal dimension in our conception of speaking the truth.

Comparable considerations operate when the Arabic verb is used of human actions other than speaking. Transitional is a phase such as *ṣadaqahu al-naṣiḥah*: a person 'was true in the advice that he gave' another person, or '. . . spoke the truth in the advice . . .', or 'advised with *ṣidq*'. Or might one not use 'right' here rather than, or certainly as well as, 'true', 'truth'? Implied is that the counsel was both sincere, and effectively wise. Non-verbally: *Ṣadaqahu al-ikhā'*, 'he was true towards him in brotherliness', or '. . . behaved towards him with true brotherhood'. Again: *ṣadaqūhum al-qitāl*, 'they fought them with *ṣidq*', 'they were true against them in battle', 'they fought against them with both genuine zeal and good effect'.

Throughout, *ṣidq* is that quality by which someone speaks or acts with a combination of inner integrity and objective overt appropriateness. It involves saying or doing the right thing out of a genuine personal recognition of its rightness, an inner alignment with it.

In modern English we have negative concepts like lying and cheating, which conceptualize overt performance in terms of the performers and their moral quality as well as in terms of the objective outward facts or rules. On the other hand, we have not developed carefully, or formulated strongly, counterpart positive concepts to assess and to interpret behaviour in these trilateral terms.[3] This is precisely what the notion *ṣadaqa* does.

Human behaviour, in word or deed, is the nexus between our inner life and the surrounding world. Truth at the personalist level is that quality by which both halves of that relationship are chaste and appropriate, are true. The Muslims were no fools when they regarded this as an important human category.

There remains yet one more move. For our relation to the truth, though intimate and integral, is not simply passive. The next step is to follow the Arabs, an activist people, into a further development of this same term, one that activates the concept and renders it transitive. For we not only hold the truth in our hearts, we also act it out.

In Arabic, as in other Semitic languages, there is a formal pattern whereby by manipulating the consonants of a root, and specifically by doubling the middle letter, a given notion is intensified, in various complicated ways, and especially is made causative.

Thus in the case at which we have been looking, from *ṣadaqa*, 'to speak the truth, to act truly, to be true', is formed *ṣaddaqa*, the so-called *tafʿīl* form: basically, 'to make come true', 'to render true'. It is an intricate causative or double transitive of wide potentiality. The verbal noun in this case is *taṣdīq*, the act or generic quality designated by the verb *ṣaddaqa*.

Let us look at this for a moment.

The simple form (*ṣadaqa*) means to say (or to do) something that is at the same time both inwardly honest and outwardly correct. What then does the reactivated form (*taṣdīq*) signify? I will list four meanings.

First: it can mean 'to regard as true'. Its primary object may be either a person, or a sentence; so that *ṣaddaqahu* or *ṣaddaqathu*, a person gave him or it *taṣdīq*, may mean a person 'held him to be a speaker of the truth', or 'held it to be spoken truly'. These might be rendered as 'believed him' (or 'it'); but in both cases it implies trust in the speaker (as 'believe' used to do in English, and for a waning number still does); it can indicate that the person that is the subject of the sentence held the other person to be *ṣādiq*, a speaker sincerely of truth on a particular occasion, or held that person to be *ṣiddīq*, an habitual teller of the truth by moral character. A translation by 'believe' is, moreover, inadequate also because it omits the reference to objective validity, since 'believe' in English has become so openly neutral a term: one can believe what is false. I have not checked enough passages to be able to affirm flatly that *taṣdīq* applies only to believing what is in fact true, and yet I think that there can be no question but that, even if there are some exceptions, the standard implication still is strongly one of objective truth as well as of sincerity. The term denotes a cosmic human quality, and does not imply sheer gullibility. Accordingly, one should translate, at this level, not by 'believe' but by 'recognize the truth of'. The difference is crucial.

Even this, however, takes care of only one side of the double reference, that to the actual correctness of what is so regarded. There is still the other side, the personal sincerity involved. This operates at least as strongly in this second form as in the first. And the personalism is of both the primary subject and the secondary: to recognize a truth as personal for others, and as personal for oneself. Thus, if I give *taṣdīq* to some statement, I not merely recognize its truth in the world outside me, and subscribe to it, but also incorporate it into my own moral integrity as a person.

A second standard usage of this form is to mean, not a person 'held him to be speaker of the truth', but rather '. . . *found* that person to be' so. One may hear someone's statement, and only subsequently find reason or experience to know that that person was no liar.

Thirdly, it may indicate this sort of notion but with a more active, resolute type of finding: that is, '. . . *proved*' the person to be a speaker of truth, or confirmed or verified the matter. Thus there is a common phrase (*ṣaddaqa al-khabara al-khabru*): 'the experience verified the report'. Accordingly, *taṣdīq* has become the term for scientific experimental verification, proving something true by test; although the notion of vindicating the experimenter as well as the experiment is never far distant. A stricter translation of the phrase just quoted would be 'the experiment verified the report and the reporter'.

Fourthly, still more deliberately, *taṣdīq* may mean to render true, to take steps to make come true. One instance of this is one's own promise: a radically important matter. Or it may apply to another's promise. Or, to another's remark. If you say that that window will be closed, and I go and close it, then I have given *taṣdīq* to you. (Recently, I came across a passage in the most basic of Muslim commentaries on the Qur'an, that of al-Tabari, where he uses the two forms of the verb in a single revealing sentence. He refers to a group of people who spoke the truth with their tongues, but did not go on to give to what they had said *taṣdīq* in their deeds.[4] We could translate here: 'They did not corroborate [or, authenticate; or, validate] their speech by their deeds.')

To summarize. *Taṣdīq* is to recognize a truth, to appropriate it, to affirm it, to confirm it, to actualize it. And the truth, in each case, is personalist and sincere.

So far what I have said has been general, and has been based primarily on the medieval Arabic dictionaries. I turn now to specifically theological interpretations. Classical Muslim thinkers, when asked what faith is, affirmed almost unanimously that it is *taṣdīq*. As an historian of religion, I have been particularly interested in various concepts of faith around the world, and this one not least. If we ponder this formula a little, and correlate it with the several versions that we have just noted of *taṣdīq*, we can see that it makes good sense, and can see what religious people meant when they said that faith is doing or making or activating truth: doing personal truth, or making truth personal.

To begin with, faith is then the *recognition* of divine truth at the personal level. Faith is the ability to recognize truth as true for oneself—and to trust it. Especially in the Islamic case, with its primarily moral orientation, this includes, or makes primary, the recognition of the authenticity and moral authority of the divine commands. Thus there is the recognition of the 'obligatoriness' of moral obligations; and the acceptance of that obligation as applying to oneself, with a personal commitment to carry it out.

Again: it is the personal making of what is cosmically true come true on earth: the *actualization* of truth (the truth about humans).

More mystically, it is the *discovery* of the truth (the personal truth) of the Islamic injunctions: the process of personal verification of them, whereby by living them out one proves them and finds that they do indeed become true, both for oneself and for the society and world in which one lives.

Taṣdīq is the inner appropriation and outward implementation of truth: the process of making or finding true in actual human life, in one's own personal spirit and overt behaviour, what God—or Reality—intends for us.

And, with many a passage strongly insisting that faith is more than knowledge, that it is a question of how one responds to the truth, one may also render the proposition 'faith is *taṣdīq*' as 'faith is the ability to trust, and to act in terms of, what one knows to be true'.

All these are not bad definitions of faith.

They are not, and are not meant to be, definitions of Islamic faith; rather, they are Islamic definitions of human faith. At issue here is not the content of faith but its form; not its object but its nature. In question is not what is true, but what one does about what is true.[5]

Let me conclude, then, this part of my presentation by summing up the Islamic vision of *ṣidq*, in its fundamentally moral and human terms. Truth, as a relation to the world, is seen as existing also in relation to us; and we are seen as acting in relation to truth.

I would now like to consider these matters in relation to modern Western society.

The transition from the one to the other may itself need clarification. First, there is the both logical and moral point that this orientation, which we have been considering from a distance, itself requires that that distance, that non-engagé objectivity and neutralist observationism, be replaced with an existential concern, a wrestling with the implications for oneself. The very suggestion that truth is not an inert and impersonal observable but that truth means truth for me, for you, is challenging. Let us face the challenge.

Secondly, more traditionally in our society, and professionally, of course, it has been the task of philosophers to deal with the concept of truth; and I am not a philosopher. I am, rather, an historian. Yet being a cultural historian is perhaps not so irrelevant as it might at first seem. At least, it explains my concern. The study of history, too, may contribute something to understanding in this realm. And vice versa: the question of truth has enormous significance for history. How truth is conceived, where it is looked for, are historical as well as theoretical issues. A comparative study of human history recognizes that different civilizations and ages have had differing visions of truth; and it must report that the choice can manifestly be of decisive consequence.

It is the cultural historian who sees how terribly important these questions can be, in the development or the disintegration of a society. The cultural historian may also see the relations between the technical philosophy of any civilization and the particular development of that civilization at a given time; and may ask whether, in the case of a society that seems, like ours, to be perhaps seriously ill, the ideas with which it is operating may be restricted within that illness. The 'ordinary language' of a society may illustrate the limitations as well as the insights of that age and that particular culture.

In any case, I am bold enough to ask whether the recent loss of a sense of the personal quality of truth may not be a serious illness. One may wonder whether the Western surrender of what seem, from a larger world perspective, to be important ingredients in human life and its awareness of reality, may not have contributed significantly to our malaise.

The concept of the truth of things I leave aside; not because it seems unimportant, but because the purpose of this present paper is to champion the personalist level of truth, and it would be distracting to complicate the argument by advocating a certain worthiness also (still?) in the realist (or if one prefer, idealist) level— although personally I am persuaded that the observations of a cultural historian in analysing what has happened to our society as a result of losing this apprehension of transcendence could be startling.

So far as personalist truth is concerned, it seems to me clear that monumental consequences have followed on our letting go of our hold on this dimension, and the resultant divorce between truth and morality. (The other loss signified a divorce in our awareness between reality and morality.) Modern Western thinkers are aware that earlier ages saw things differently, or at least spoke of things differently; but they tend to leave aside social consequences, and to believe on purely theoretical grounds that the divorces have constituted an advance in clarity. I am less interested in clarity than in truth and goodness; and I have a suspicion that the world is in fact more complicated, especially in its interconnections and in our relations to it, than modern theories sometimes allow for.

Not that we have lost this apprehension totally. As with the truth of things, so also here for personalist truth, the modern Western world does preserve remnants of an older orientation in a few of its phrases. We speak of a person being true to her word, of course, but also true to his wife, or true to her office. Or we may say that, given his responsibilities, he acted falsely. And apparently the word 'true' is originally cognate with 'trust' (and 'troth').

These kinds of truth and falsity, however, are not much investigated in the modern university.

It is possible to discern a long-range development that has been taking place. Greatly to oversimplify, one may perhaps aphorize that, in our Western tradition, the notion of the truth of things is Platonic, that of the truth of propositions Aristotelian. Platonism is no longer strong in our day, of course (some would add, alas). Aristotle is hardly to be taxed, however, with recent extreme developments of the other tendency, and particularly the current emphasis on specifically impersonal propositions.

This latter emphasis has perhaps not had such serious effects in the realm of the natural sciences, where it began; but we must ask whether it does not become a more serious problem when first social scientists, and then philosophers, follow. (One realizes that one is taking on quite an array of authorities, then, when one questions the development!) Natural scientists deliberately and with success strive to construct impersonal statements, sentences whose meaning and whose truth are both independent of the one who makes them. And they see the truth of a statement as, in large measure, precisely a function of its impersonality. Involved in this has been the rise—and of course the brilliant, indeed spectacular, success—of the objective method, of relentless analysis (as distinct from synthesis), and of all that we know as scientific.

In the study of the natural world, this seems to do not only much good, but concomitantly little harm; although recently both nuclear weapons and ecological problems raise a new question of whether even in the natural sciences the amoral, impersonal approach is quite so unchallengeable as one used to think.

However that may be, it is not difficult to argue that applying this approach in other areas of inquiry has been imitative at best, disastrous at worst, and, one might suggest, perhaps illegitimate throughout. I particularly wish to query the theory that it is legitimate or helpful to regard truth, and falsity, as pertaining to statements considered apart from the person who makes them or about whom they are made.

There are some statements, of course, whose truth, and indeed whose meaning, turn, and are meant to turn, on the question of who says them: statements such as 'I am twenty years old', which is false if I make it but true if someone else does. Now it is of course possible to construct special ways of dealing with these so as to avoid, or at least adequately to handle, the problems that are involved. It is also possible, of course, to translate all such statements into more manageable impersonalisms, although I am not sure that this is a healthy impetus. There are some extremely important sentences of this sort, such as 'I love you'.[6]

To elaborate this point, let me turn from propositions to games. I should like to reflect upon a game of basketball. First, however, in order to set up an analogy, let me recall the Arabic usage that we considered earlier: 'They fought with *ṣidq*'. Now a counterpart to that idea is preserved in our modern colloquial: 'That was a real battle!' I find it interesting to reflect on the case of a basketball game that turns out to have been rigged—so that the players were only pretending to compete, while in fact they were deceptively, perhaps with great skill, going through the motions of the contest and actually contriving to achieve a previously determined (and paid-for) result. Now, popularly, such a contest would not be called 'a real game'. In this I find evidence that, despite the prevalence of strict positivistic empiricism, and despite an intellectual formulation of that mood philosophically, in fact our society preserves here some remnants of a stand that interprets even the objective world, and assesses its facts, in terms of the moral integrity of the participants. In this instance it is not merely the personal character of the players that is being judged according to moral criteria, but the nature of the observable events. The set of actual (observable) activities in two cases could be identical: yet it would be affirmed that the moral qualities of the actors determined whether what was taking place is in one case 'a game' and in the other case 'not a true game', or, even, not a game at all.

Or, putting the point in more linguistic terms, we may say that many of us choose to use the concept 'game' in such a way that it applies only when certain moral factors are operative, and does not apply when these are removed. (Admittedly, one can usually take them for granted.) I hope that the point will not seem blunted by such a shift to language. It is a matter of conceptualization: not simply of how one speaks, but of how one sees and interprets the world, and how one relates oneself to it. The cultural historian might well report that something has been lost in the course of a society's development when that society, let us say in the name of objectivity, has ceased to discriminate, in its language and thought, between a game that is rigged and one that is not.

Similarly, as a cultural historian I venture to wonder whether a society has not lost something of major significance once it decides to think of the truth and falsity of statements independently of human and moral involvements. It can be done, of course, as our culture shows. Yet the price one pays is high, as our culture also shows.

Let me not try to persuade, however, so much as to elucidate. In terms of understanding, may we not formulate this equation: that those who can appreciate what is meant by saying that a rigged sports event is not a true game, will be in a position to apprehend what is denoted by the Arabic word ṣadaqa.[7]

A statement, similarly, might be exactly the same in two cases, but whether that statement is to be called 'true' (ṣidq) or not would depend not only on its content but also on the moral intent and involvement with which it is said.[8]

Further, I am propounding the suggestion that our society may have arrived historically at a point in its academic and much of its cultural life, with regard to its notion of truth and its activities relating to that notion, where a society would be in its sports life if it had decided to use the same concept, and perhaps act in the same way, concerning basketball, regardless of cheating.

That something has gone wrong with our notion of truth is beginning to be suspected also in academia. A question about what sort of thing truth is has come to haunt the modern university. Student turmoil may be discerned as in part a deep though inchoate restlessness about the particular concept of truth that of late, and almost surreptitiously, has come to prevail; or perhaps rather, about an inarticulately felt absence of alternative concepts. In particular, an unreality, and an impersonalism, are sensed in much of what passes for truth in what the university is engaged in pursuing: a lack of correlation either with absolute significance, with an ultimate, on the one hand, or on the other hand with the inner integrity and wholeness of those persons who are invited to pursue it.

Might we reflect together a little on what kind of transformation might be involved if in a university a personalist conception of truth were to replace the current amoral and impersonal one? Let us take the case of a journal article. For the sake of simplicity we may suppose that it is in some field other than the natural sciences, even though I am not fully sure that we should exclude them. In the social sciences and the humanities, anyway, I feel more confident to speak.

What are we to mean in saying that this article is or is not true?

First, we all agree that such a judgement is concerned with the content of the article, with what it says. Does what it says correspond to the facts, to use traditional phrasing (used also by Austin, I find)? Is it related to the empirical world in an objective, verifiable way? Is it objectively true, by whatever modern standard for this one chooses?

On this, as I say, all agree, and I discuss it no further. Let me emphasize, however, that this does not mean that I consider it unimportant. I stress its significance and its indispensability; we move on simply because it is not controversial. I take it fully for granted.

Many would discuss nothing else. The modern university in general, as well as many modern logicians in particular, are content with this particular dimension of the matter, whatever the pluralism in how it is to be analysed or formulated. The criteria by which this is to be judged, the meaning that it shall have, are questions that we need not settle; we all simply agree that this area of truth is at stake. My suggestion is that there are other additional areas, involving additional criteria and meanings of a quite different sort, that might profitably be brought into play.

For instance: with a personalist concept of truth, the article, no matter what it said, would be regarded as not true if it had been published by someone primarily to get a promotion, or even a reputation.[9]

Thirdly, it could be regarded as not true if it studied human or social affairs without recognizing the personalist level of truth in what was being studied. (This is one of our meanings of *taṣdīq*, one may recall.) A researcher who has ferreted out facts and established them (*muḥaqqiq*), or a commentator who has made sound (*ṣaḥīḥ*) but impersonal reports about them, as academics are sometimes content to do, would in this orientation be regarded as not having written a *true* article.

In my field of Orientalist studies, there is a type of research practised by remote observers, chiefly Westerners writing only or in principle for a Western audience. In this type of study, the outsider's formulations are never meant to be checked by Asians to see whether the impersonal, so-called objectivist truths are also existentially true, or can become so, in terms of those Asians' personal lives. Similarly, in the 'behavioural' sciences one gets writing whose truth is not calculated for testing by being experimentally subjected to personal verification by those being written about. All writing about human affairs that is formulated only for one's peers would come under this stricture.

A counterpart for the social sciences and humanities of the verificationist principle in the natural sciences is the principle that no statement about human affairs is true that cannot be existentially appropriated by those about whom the statement is made.[10]

Finally, no statement might be accepted as true that had not been inwardly appropriated by its author. Studies of that impersonalist kind whose truths make no difference to the moral character of the one who deals with them, would be rejected. I have met psychologists who tell me, and without any sheepish embarrassment, that they use determinism as an intellectual hypothesis in their academic work, without necessarily or in fact living their own lives on the determinist principle. For a university or a journal editor to decide not to treat the writing of such authors as false, is a major decision.[11]

It might be felt absurdly utopian even to speculate about so radical a transformation of current academic thinking. That is to overlook, I feel, the depth of our present crisis. Human integrity cannot be dismissed as too high a price to pay for reform. Student protest, in all its destructive vehemence, has little vision of a better world and yet is not altogether amiss in feeling that something has gone seriously wrong with the academic world, the intellectual system. It talks of restructuring the university whereas the significant flaw, I would contend, is not in structures, in organizational patterns, in 'where power lies', and in other such relatively superficial matters. Rather, it is the ideas dominating and informing our intellectual life that have somehow gone awry; specifically, I am suggesting, the idea that truth can be truly seen as amoral and impersonal.

Those not persuaded of the alternative, personalist position will see two points at issue here: the moral, on the one hand, and the theoretical. In the end, I would argue that the impersonal orientation is intellectually untenable. At a more proximate level, however, one need not suggest that it is logically incoherent. It is far from obviously impossible to construct a total intellectual system, theoretically self-consistent, within which this logic can serve. My thesis is rather, in the first instance, that to choose that system, rather than a more personalist one, is a decision that a society makes, or that we personally make. And it is a fateful decision. To see it so is not simply a personal judgement, but an historical observation. My suggestion is that the system has worked well in the natural sciences (even though that era may be coming to an end) but that it works badly in human affairs.

The history of religion reminds us that total intellectual systems, of great sophistication, power, and elegance, have been constructed for the Islamic, for the medieval Christian, for the monist Hindu, and for other positions; there is no great reason to doubt that comparably consistent systems for amoral propositionalism can be built. History reminds us too that the social and personal consequences of living in accord with any of those systems have been impressively diverse. It is possible to study, and interesting to discover, what those consequences are.

At this level, then, my thesis is not the logical one that a given system in contemporary Western culture is not self-consistent or even (in the short run) operationally competent. Rather, it is the cultural historian's thesis that personal and social consequences of mighty proportions are implicit in the orientation that one chooses.

More positively, since the alternative view of truth being pro-pounded inescapably involves morality, one way of formulating the thesis is to say: It is better to see truth as personal. Or per-haps: We ought to see truth thus.

And, although I have, on the whole, left aside the natural sci-ences in my survey, it is clear that a serious question is being force-fully pressed about war research and the morality of science in general; even though that question has not been much formulated philosophically, I believe. I am inclined to wonder whether a for-mulation might not be fruitful in terms of a convergence between personal morality and objective truth.[12]

Yet there remains one phenomenon on our campuses that can be subsumed, I believe, under this same heading. This is the reaction against the establishment, in the name of personalistic 'honesty'. A great to-do has been made in terms of honesty, in ways that seem to me not to solve our society's problem at this level so much as to illustrate it—and even perhaps to exacerbate it.

It is intrepid and may seem callous to criticize the notion of honesty these days, since it seems about all that many people have left of their humanity. Yet I think that here too the unification[13] of sincerity and objective rightness is sorely needed. The ideal is per-sonal truth, as I have been contending; but personal truth (ṣidq) is an integration in which is involved more than impersonal truth but more also than honesty. For the way to hell is paved with good intentions; just as is the way to Hiroshima or to bacteriological warfare with good objective science.

There is more to the virtue of personalized truth than mere outward propriety or correctness, as I have been arguing all along; yet there is more also than mere sincerity or well-meaning inten-tion. There is no room here for that kind of truth that leaves unaf-fected the moral character and private behaviour of those who know it. Equally, there is none of that modern nonsense whereby one has simply to unbottle one's emotions, whatever they be, so that feelings are to be expressed regardless of consequences or pro-priety, or so that we come close to hearing that it is honest to tell a lie provided that one really wants to tell it.

Ṣidq rejects hypocrisy, resoundingly. Yet equally it rejects solipsism and irresponsibility.

If objective truth is not inherently or ideally or conceptually linked with personal life, then personal life is thought of as not to be linked with objective truth, or indeed with any standards. A price that we have paid for divorcing objective truth from sincerity, is to divorce subjective emotionalism from all discipline—and from community cohesion. We have made truth amoral; the next generation has made self-expression amoralistic also. This makes for social disorder, and for personal loneliness, and lostness. Just as we cannot have a basketball game without honesty, so there can be none without rules. It is a sorry society whose only two activities seem to be organized dishonest contests on the one hand and chaotic, fragmentedly private, bacchanalia on the other.

But of course life is not a game, it is 'for real'. The rules of life must be objectively true—as well as personally right.

Over against the historical argument, some would respond, the theoretical horn of our dilemma remains. It might be 'better' to live in a world of personalist truth: better for us as persons, better for our society, better even for our universities as institutions. Yet if it not be 'truer', then we ought not to choose its comfort over the bleakness, demanding all our courage, of the world as it starkly, impersonally, is.

This consideration is important; and, if the dichotomy were valid, my own commitment to truth is such that I too would choose it. (Does this mean, then, that one cannot after all, in dealing with the theoretical issue of what truth is, escape wrestling with the metaphysical issue of what Reality [*haqq*] is, as well as the moral issue, as to how one shall personally relate to both? Is it possible, within a logical system that repudiates metaphysical and moral dimensions to truth, to assert that one concept of truth is either truer, or better, than another?) This very consideration, in any case, of whether one should choose truth over comforting illusion, itself begins to bridge the gulf between truth and moral integrity. For the commitment to truth is personal, is moral.

Besides, our argument is not at all that one should choose personal morality rather than objective truth. Those who see the locus of truth and falsity as statements or propositions, are not contending that the only criterion of truth is logical self-consistency. The formulation must be internally coherent, no doubt; but, to be true, it must also relate to objective facts in a certain strict fashion. Similarly, to see the locus of truth and falsity as persons is not to contend that honesty or internal integrity is the sole criterion. When truth is seen as personal, a person's statement must not only cohere with his or her (and if it be about other persons, then also with their) inner life, but must also relate to objective facts in that same exacting fashion.

Moreover, the choice that we make is not quite ours to make arbitrarily. Even if it could be shown theoretically that personalist and propositional conceptions of truth were equally plausible (although I do not believe that they are), there are other factors involved. A university that I served has as its motto: *Veritas.* It is cheating a little, the historian may report, if to-day it interprets that aspiration as towards merely propositional truth, when the word once meant, and Harvard once meant by it, a truth from which health and wholeness and integrity are not precluded. Thus we are not quite at liberty to make the term 'truth' mean whatever we choose to mean by it; for we are trustees in our society of traditions and values and even of terms whose moral as well as intellectual content is at stake. A university unconcerned with personal truth is 'untrue' to the academic tradition, historically, as well as sadly partial in its apprehension of intellectual rigour to-day.

For the conceptual systems that we adopt do themselves, in their entirety, like individual statements within them, have to be related to the world in which we live, and not merely to be internally consistent. The medieval Islamic, Christian, Hindu Weltanschauungen were once mighty orientations but to-day they serve no longer so well because, however coherent in themselves and however true to personal inner life, they have not incorporated (cannot incorporate?) into their structures the new data of modern scientific and historical knowledge. Similarly the conceptual system of amoral propositionalism, however logically potent, cannot successfully cope with the data, the givenness, of human moral and personal life. A conception of truth that is impersonal handles the natural world well, but comprehends the human world ineptly.

My presentation may not have succeeded in making persuasive the suggestion that advance in our individual and corporate life requires a personalization of our sense of truth, a reintegration of objective rightness and inward rightness. At least I am grateful for the opportunity of arguing for an awareness that little is so important about a culture, or a century, or a person, as her, his or its vision of truth. Pilate's unanswered question, What is Truth? whether expressed or latent, haunts every civilization, and finally, I guess, every man, woman and child. We may hope that our society will not cease to wrestle with it earnestly and nobly. In such wrestling, even if we be maimed by it, there may surely be a blessing.

CHAPTER 8

Objectivity and the Humane Sciences: A New Proposal

In this chapter I will set forth one idea, which I shall endeavour to propound, to elucidate, and to defend. In one sense it is a relatively simple idea; yet I am well aware that it is radical, and ramifying. To advocate its adoption is, at the present juncture of intellectual evolution in academia, to propose no minor development; it is advanced here in the conviction, however, that the time has come for a major new departure, a new vision. Given the depth of our contemporary crisis, both in our civilization and in the university, that the idea is in some ways drastic seems not necessarily a weakness.

In my title I have used the phrase 'humane sciences'. By this I mean all study of persons by persons. The current fashion has been to pattern intellectual activity in the university into three or four realms: the natural sciences, plus perhaps the life sciences; the social sciences; and the humanities. It is the last two that concern us here. The division between them has indeed become more than a fashion, with its practical institutionalization, and its theoretical and as well deep emotional involvements—although in the French language, and on the Continent generally, the dichotomy is not so sharp as in the English-speaking world. The phrasing 'humane sciences' is apt in so far as it may suggest a superseding of that dichotomizing within the study of human affairs, and may suggest also a certain continuity (but emphatically not sameness) between our study of the objective world of nature, in 'the sciences', and our study of those human affairs; between, that is, our study of the external world of things, and our study of ourselves.

My phrase 'humane sciences' is not simply a translation from the French. For one thing, central to my thesis is a discrimination between the concepts of human knowing and humane knowing. Our knowledge of the material world is human knowledge, since it is we who have it. It is our knowledge of *the human* that I am calling humane knowledge—that is, knowledge of persons by persons. All science is human science. All knowing is by humans. Incidentally, therefore, I would quarrel with Sir Karl Popper's notion of objective knowledge, although it would take us too far afield to pursue that question here, or the differences between his views and Polanyi's. For the moment, I would simply make clear my thesis. It is of importance for my argument—although I would hold, of importance also for the health of our civilization, and for the future of humankind—to recognize that the natural sciences are human sciences, in the sense of human activities, human products: they constitute knowledge and study on the part of humans. Knowledge and study by humans of the non-human are one thing; humane sciences, on the other hand, are knowledge and study of persons by persons.

I personally am a humanist, in more than one sense of the word; not incidentally but committedly, not passively but as an active champion of humanist values as indispensable to the whole university as an institution, and at the theoretical level to all of knowledge, to all knowing, as a human activity. On taking up a new appointment at Harvard some years ago, however, I discovered myself formally categorized within a social sciences division; and certainly I hold it manifest that to understand humanity is to understand the human as social. I hold it manifest also that an understanding of human society does not deserve to be called scientific if it omits the characteristically humane: if it does not see and interpret society as human in the fullest, deepest, most transcendent sense. Also, of course, it does not deserve to be called scientific unless it is ruthlessly rigorous, critical, rational. We have then hardly yet attained humane sciences in these senses; hence our fragmentation. It is in the hopes of contributing towards such attainment that I make bold to proffer my suggestion.

It involves—dare I admit it?—a moving beyond the goal of objectivity. Please do not get up and walk out at this point: I am conscious that it will at first blush seem offensive to many of you to hear that sacred symbol of scientific and rational thought being irreverently considered and critically scrutinized—and assessed as rationally inadequate in this field. Yet I am inviting you, not to a simple rejection of it, but to go beyond it. If you are kind enough to stay and hear me out, I am hopeful that my argument may emerge as constructive, and even helpful; as rational, and even scientific—as well as humane.

I know of no careful study, historical, critical, self-conscious, of the concept of objectivity in the history of Western thought. Yet I think it safe to affirm two or three propositions. One is that objectivity has been regarded as not merely characteristic of, but foundational for, scientific knowledge. Secondly, the alternative to the objective has been thought to be the subjective. I am proposing that these two observations, although both valid so far as they go, are first approximations, only, to the truth; and I suggest that we have reached a point where we both must, and can, move beyond them.

So far as the first is concerned, I would submit that objectivity is the correct, scientific way of dealing intellectually with objects; but that it must be supplemented when what is to be known is other than, or more than, an object—for instance, is a person, or a work of art, or a tribe. I contend that to treat a person as if he or she were an object, or anything pertaining to the human as if it were only an object, besides being immoral, is to misunderstand him or her or it; that it constitutes an intellectual error. Accordingly, since more essentially characteristic of, foundational for, scientific procedure is the use of concepts appropriate for what is being studied, I contend that it is pseudo-scientific, is scientific in only an imitative and not a genuine sense, to apply to the study of human affairs the objectivity that is appropriate for the study of other fields. To claim that a procedure or a conceptual pattern is scientific, one must do more than demonstrate that it has been fruitful in a quite different area of study.

So far as the second proposition is concerned, the subjective/objective polarity, I submit that in addition to the subjective, my individual and internalist awareness of something or someone, or of myself, and to the objective, the impersonal, externalist knowledge, there is a third position which subsumes both of these and goes beyond them; and that it is this that we should posit as our goal, in the humane field, the study of persons by persons. I call it critical corporate self-consciousness.

A third characterization of objectivity is that an observer's knowledge of a given object is in principle available also and equally to any other observer—ideally, to all humankind. By corporate self-consciousness I intend knowledge that is in principle available both to the subject him- or herself, and to all external observers; or in the case of group activities, to both outside observers and to participants. Again, this means in principle all humankind. We shall be returning later to the logical flaw, and the consequent distortion of knowledge, involved in the fact that the ideal of objective knowledge of the human is in principle limited, not universal—since it is confined to outsiders.

The transition from consciousness to self-consciousness is one of the profound, crucial moments in human evolution. Its first appearance represents the emergence of the human. The transition from consciousness to critical consciousness was another extraordinary moment, marking the appearance of science, and its expanding development. The emergence of critical self-consciousness is the major transition through which the human race is perhaps now about to go. Science, our spectacularly successful intellectual achievement, will expand from the world of nature to the world of our own selves; and, moreover, our awareness about ourselves and our neighbour will expand to become truly scientific, truly rational; not when our knowledge of the human is objective, which is theoretically inapt and practically disruptive, but rather when human self-consciousness becomes fully critical and fully corporate, ideally embracing us all both in our diversity and in our personalism.

We are talking about the study of persons by persons. By corporate critical self-consciousness I mean that critical, rational, inductive self-consciousness by which a community of persons, constituted at a minimum by two persons, the one being studied and the one studying, but ideally by the whole human race, is aware of any given particular human condition or action as a condition or action of itself as a community, yet of one part but not of the whole of itself; and is aware of it as it is experienced and understood simultaneously both subjectively (personally, existentially) and objectively (externally, critically, analytically; as one used to say, scientifically).

Introduced here is a decisive new principle of verification. The intellectual pursuit in humane studies of corporate self-consciousness, critical, rational, empirical, is scientific in various senses; including that of its being subject, and its alone being subject, in the deepest sense, to a valid verification procedure. In objective knowledge, that a first observer's understanding has done justice to what is observed is testable by the experience of a second and third observer. In corporate critical self-consciousness, that justice has been done to the matter being studied is testable by the experience of the subject or subjects. Often the former—another observer—is in principle not available; since unlike what obtains in the world of matter, no human situation is truly repeatable. In any case, it is inadequate; partly because all observers are inherently less than the whole of humankind (a point to which we will return), and partly because it is intrinsic to human experience that that experience appears differently, and in fact *is* different, from the inside and from without. No statement involving persons is valid, I propose, unless its validity can be verified both by the persons involved and by critical observers not involved.

I will illustrate what kind of thing I mean by all this in a moment; as I have said, the second part of my presentation is to elucidate my thesis. Meanwhile, let me state it, simply.

In a sentence, then, my proposal is that all humane knowledge—all knowledge of persons by persons—is in principle a form of self-consciousness. More historically: we have reached a point where we can, and, I suggest, must, recognize this, and choose it. The proper goal of humane knowing, then, the ideal to which we should aspire academically, scientifically, is not objectivity but corporate critical self-consciousness. My submission is that this will yield truer knowledge; that with anything less we betray intellectual accuracy. Negatively, in this realm merely objective knowledge, like merely subjective knowledge, inherently involves major error, and the pursuit of it is irrational. It is also potentially immoral, and destructive, although that is not here my point. Positively, this new definition of our aim opens up enormously rich rewards of understanding (this can be demonstrated empirically), and—that matter of no small importance—of valid verification.

There is time in this presentation to develop the positive proposal only slightly. Obviously it is a major matter. Given the general title of this symposium, however, much of my argument here will be critical, rather: that, as an ideal in this field, objectivity is wrong.

My argument rests both on theoretical considerations and on empirical observations. At the former level, of rational analysis, the basic premises of my thesis are two. The first is that the human is patently different, in ways highly significant, from material objects, and from all other forms of life known to us; so that any ideas about the human that underestimate our uniqueness or downplay our humanity are *prima facie* inadequate, or worse. Human qualities such as self-transcendence, a sense of justice, a creative and destructive imagination, a capacity to respond to and to create beauty, a capacity for wickedness and also for dignity, freedom, compassion, rationality; a cunning capacity to deceive and also a drive or aspiration towards intellectual and moral integrity; the pursuit of truth; a sense of remorse, an ability to forgive; moral responsibility; and so on and on and on: these are manifest facts; and, frankly, it strikes me as rather stupid either to propound or to put up with theories that, whether in their presuppositions or in their conclusions, or often both, fail to do justice to these facts. The advocates of such theories, when challenged, usually fall back for defence on the plea that their theories, however seemingly absurd or inhumane, are 'scientific'; which succeeds only in giving science a bad name.

The second premise is the equally inescapable one that the knowing mind is human; is not outside, and cannot get outside, the human race to look at it externally, objectively. This has long been recognized as a difficulty, in objectivist theories; but it has been regarded also as a regrettable weakness, and attempts have been made to reduce its significance as far as possible, to approach as closely as feasible to externalized viewing. I, on the other hand, regard the participation of the knowing mind in the humanity that it seeks to know as an asset, and not merely an inescapable fact; and I would order our intellectual inquiry in accord with it, not in opposition to it nor in flight from it. My reason is simple: that it helps us to know.

The empirical observations on which my position rests have had to do primarily with a field of study with which I have been myself involved for forty years: namely, cross-cultural inquiry, and specifically the Western academic study of the Orient and especially of its religious history. The position that I am propounding is, I maintain, of quite general relevance. The validity of the position, however, has been rendered primarily conspicuous in both the successes and the failures evident in the endeavour of one civilization to understand another. The limitations and indeed the fallacies of both the subjective and objective types of knowledge have here become clear; as well as the enormously rich potential of the new transcultural critical self-consciousness.

Accordingly, I will draw illustrative material from this realm, but will endeavour to go on to suggest the general applicability.

In Western understanding of, let us say, India, there has been a clear advance through successive stages: first, ignorance; secondly, impressionistic awareness of random parts of the culture (an outside subjective stage); thirdly, a growingly systematic and accurate yet insensitive and externalist knowledge of facts (an objective stage); and, more recently, and richly promising, the beginnings of serious and even profound humane understanding of the role and meaning of those facts in the lives and the culture of the persons involved. (This last carries strikingly forward, in some cases almost transforms, India's own self-awareness, the erstwhile insider's subjective knowledge.)

I call this last stage personalist. I hope that it is hardly necessary to insist that by 'personal' I do not mean 'individual'. Personality is profoundly social. The opposite of individual is social; the opposite of personal is impersonal. The earlier stage was of an impersonal knowledge of facts (it aimed at impersonal knowledge). The newer stage is of a personal knowledge, and understanding, of the meaning of those facts, in the cultural life of Indians. It generates statements about Indian life that both Indians and outside observers can jointly recognize as true, and illuminating.

The successive stages of this process can be demonstrated both for the total systems of the religio-cultural complexes which Westerners objectified by giving them names such as 'Hinduism', 'Islam', and also for each particular item within those complexes. The former is in some ways more interesting, but too sophisticated a matter to go into here.

Let us look, rather, not at the over-all pattern but at a particular item within it. Recently I had occasion to visit the South Indian city of Madurai, site of a famous and magnificent temple. Again, Western awareness of this temple has gone through the same stages: from ignorance, through impressionistic travellers' tales of its sumptuousness and grandeur, and then through a meticulous and detailed knowledge of the temple as an object of observation (it has, for instance, among other glories a hall of several hundred pillars, on any one of which a descriptive analysis of the intricate art work could constitute a Ph.D. dissertation topic). I had never been that far south in India before, and I was entranced to observe the temple, in which I spent many hours. It is an interesting question, however, as to what it is at which one looks when visiting a sacred structure. More engaging than the temple itself were persons worshipping within it and their worship. Or we may say, the important matter was the living complex constituted by the temple and the worshippers within it.

The truth of the temple manifestly lay not in the building itself as an object but in its significance for, and interaction with, these men and women. The temple primarily is what it is perceived by them as being; or at the least, their perception of it is incontrovertibly part of its truth. Recent Western understanding of the temple has gone forward dramatically as scholars have come to recognize that the role of such a temple in the consciousness and the lives of persons is part of what one must know if one sets out to know the facts. It is out of Hindu religious consciousness that the temple arose in the first place, and in that consciousness that its reality primarily continues to lie.

Actually, in this particular case there never was a time when Westerners' apprehension of the building was merely and totally objective; since if it had been so, they would not even have recognized it as a temple. The most rank outsider always participated in Hindu consciousness to at least *that* extent. The notion of temple, and that of symbol in general, are humane concepts, not objective. No building is objectively a temple. No space is objectively sacred. No object is objectively a symbol, in and of itself: an object becomes a symbol in the consciousness of certain persons.

To have merely objective knowledge of what serves some people or a certain community symbolically is to misunderstand it; this kind of undiscerning knowledge has in historical fact distorted, and at times indeed vitiated, outsiders' observations in this realm.

That a given object symbolizes one thing for one group of people, something else for another group, and perhaps nothing at all for a third group, is a fact without which human history would have been dramatically different from what it has been and is.

Merely objective knowledge not merely fails to illuminate, for instance, religious conflict, but actually has often contributed to it. The only knowledge that is accurate of the history of religion, and indeed of culture, and indeed of human history generally, is a knowledge that participates in the consciousness of those involved.

To understand a symbol, I am contending, one must both know it objectively and in addition know what it means, has meant, in the lives and consciousness (including the subconsciousness) of persons. This varies, of course, from community to community, and from age to age. It is never quite precise: like a poem, only much more so, it shimmers with a whole range of meanings, and of innuendos—overt, subtle, and hidden, conscious and unconscious, quiescent or activating. Moreover, it is not simply what the symbol itself means to persons, but what life means, what the universe means, in the light of that symbol. My own studies have led me to the view that a symbol in principle never means exactly the same thing to any two persons (nor even necessarily to any one person at different times); although on this both Jung and Eliade, two of the greatest twentieth-century scholars in this realm, have tended to presume otherwise, without, I feel, having thought the matter through. We need not go into that issue here, beyond my indicating that as an historian I am inescapably aware of diversity and change. In any case there is no dispute but that the meaning of things in human history lies in their relation to persons, in the interaction of human beings with them, and not in themselves as objects.

An objective knowledge of the moon, provided by natural science, is different from, and for humane studies is less than, a knowledge of the role of the moon in human life and in the history of human culture and poetry and religion and love; and even in the history of human science and technology and space travel. The natural sciences cannot tell us about the moon all that we want to know, or that is worth knowing. Let us not be so fatuous as to forget this massive fact.

I would go further, and insist that the role of the moon, or of the temple of the moon in ancient Babylon, or of that temple of Minaksi in Madurai, in the consciousness and the lives of men, women, and children—that is, their role in human history: what they have meant and signified and been and done—is not fully nor even accurately knowable by behavioural sciences either, which are externalistic and explicitly leave out of consideration the self-consciousness of those involved. To understand the human, and to understand history, it is necessary to know not only what we do, the behaviourist's little province, but what we refrain from doing, what we dream of doing, what we fear to do; what we do with exultation, hesitation, guilt, or boredom. An action is not understood unless one discerns what courage went into it, what routine, what integrity or duplicity, what choice. To read a statement in a Sanskrit or Arabic text one must know what it says but also what it takes for granted. One must listen to what people leave unsaid, be sensitive to their failures, recognize what they do in terms of what they are trying to do. As Dilthey long ago insisted, the behaviour of human beings is to be seen and interpreted as within a context of the consciousness that gives meaning to their lives and to that behaviour.

Fundamentally, one makes a rather stupid historian if one fails to recognize that other people are in fact human beings like ourselves. This statement seems so obvious, and so innocent, and yet the depth of our academic crisis lies in the fact that it is so radical. If one does not see and feel that the people whom one studies are human beings like oneself; and if as teacher and scholar one does not enable one's students and one's readers to see and to feel it, then one has failed as an historian, has failed to arrive at knowledge. If you wish to call this kind of humane knowledge 'unscientific', I do not much mind; I would rather be on the right track than orthodox. But by this kind of conformism you have merely legislated limits to the capacity of science to know—unnecessarily and foolishly. There are things in human consciousness waiting to be known, things of enormous significance for all of us; and some of us are resolved to know them, and have devised methods and procedures and understandings for knowing them and for making them known. It is true that these things are not objects, and cannot be known objectively; but they are real, and can be known accurately, verifiably, humanely. It is the task of the humane sciences to know them and to make them known.

What is involved in doing this we are only now beginning to realize, however. My presentation to-day is itself part of our endeavour to become self-conscious as to what we are doing in this important realm.

To return to that Madurai temple. I remarked earlier that from the very beginning outside observers went beyond mere objectivity to knowing that it was indeed a temple. Their notion of what a temple is, however, was limited and inadequate; in some cases, distorted. Some Christians, some secularists, had a quite imperceptive or false sense of Hindu religious life, even though they were not unaware that it existed and was important. It is worth noting that even now, despite a great deal of progress in this realm, so that our understanding of temples in general and of this one in particular is vastly richer, deeper, truer, than was theirs, nonetheless it is still the case to-day that no one on earth, neither Hindu nor outsider, yet fully knows what a temple is. No one fully understands what it means, in human life and in cosmic life, that that building is 'a temple' for those persons. Our knowledge of templeness, if I may coin a term, is much better than it was; yet it is by no means complete.

To appreciate the significance of that temple as a temple, we must get inside the consciousness of those for whom it is a sacred space, must know how it feels and what it means to be a worshipper within it; although we must also know all the objective facts about it; and as well, in order to know the full truth about the temple, we must know its significance in the lives of shopkeepers in its environment, must know its crucial role in the whole city life and the town plan of Madurai (on which my son, an architect, has done some work), and must know how it is perceived also by the small iconoclastic Muslim group in the area, for whom temple worship is a sin, and how it is perceived by atheists and by Marxists, whose analysis of its economic role is impertinent in one sense but not in both.

True knowledge of this temple as a human institution, as a reality in the life of several millions of persons, must incorporate its role in the consciousness of worshippers within it as well as of critical observers on the outside, in so far as each is valid. The insiders, if they are dedicated to full knowledge, full self-consciousness, must and ideally will incorporate into their awareness the truth that outsiders see, so far as it be true; and the external observers, if they are resolute to attain to true knowledge, must incorporate into their understanding not only their critical analyses from the outside, in all their rigour, but also the reality that the temple constitutes in the life of the pious devotee, which after all is the primary reality of the temple as a fact in human affairs. There is no theoretical reason why these two persons, and indeed why all human beings whatever who may direct their attention to this temple, should not ideally converge in synthesizing all this truth into one conceptual apprehension. This would then constitute what I am calling corporate critical self-consciousness: with all of us recognizing in full awareness that some of us worship in this temple and some of us look on. This, and not the outsiders' partial knowledge, is, I am suggesting, the ideal at which to aim for human knowledge of that particular reality.

When at the beginning of last century the early Christian missionary Bishop Heber, who had almost no understanding of Hindu spirituality, said that Hindu 'idolaters' 'bow down to sticks and stones', he was objectively right, but, I would argue, scientifically wrong. At least, he was humanely wrong. For he failed to participate in the consciousness of those whom he was observing; or to realize that that consciousness was part of the truth of what he was looking at. They bowed down not to the sticks and stones, but before what these symbolized to them. In his externalist observation, Heber was a forerunner of modern behavioural scientists; like them, although in one sense what he said was true though misleading, in a much more significant sense he just did not know what he was talking about.

Any objectivist, externalist, behaviourist observer who leaves out human consciousness simply does not know what he or she is talking about. This applies equally to my former colleague at Harvard, Skinner, and to that early missionary.

For these matters may be generalized, throughout the comparative study of the history of religion, through the whole range of comparative culture, and finally, I am suggesting, to the entire humane field. The truth of anything that pertains to the human lies, and has always lain, not merely in that thing, but in our involvement with it; and in the end, in our involvement through it, with ourselves, with our neighbour, and with God—or with the universe *in toto*.

As I have said before, to understand the faith of Buddhists, one must look not at something called 'Buddhism'. Rather, one must look at the world—so far as possible, through Buddhist eyes.

In order to do that, one must know the data of what I have called the Buddhist tradition, at a particular time and place; must know the facts that to that person were religiously significant. The tradition at any given moment is observable, is concrete, is objective. It can, therefore, and must, therefore, be studied objectively. This requires the utmost rigour of scholarly exactitude: meticulous care, scrupulous precision, and erudite attention to minutiae. All this is needed in order to reconstruct, in the strictest factual accuracy, what the tradition historically was (has been, is).

This inescapable first step is, however, only the first step: the one who takes it is an historian of a religious tradition, not yet an historian of religion. For this is *human* history. The faith of a Buddhist does not lie in the data of the Buddhist tradition. To apprehend it, one must know where to look. The locus of faith is persons. The tradition came into existence in the first place, and survived, and developed, as an element in the life of human beings; and we have understood it, intellectually, academically, truly, only in so far as we can see human lives in terms of it, can see the significance that the data had for men, for women, and for children, and the meaning that life had for them because of those data. That significance, that meaning, the role of these data in their lives—not only in their overt behaviour but in their aspirations and their fears, their imagination and their embarrassment, their self-understanding—these are not an object and cannot be known objectively.

Yet they can be known, more or less accurately. To apprehend them requires interpretation, imagination, insight, perceptivity, human sympathy, humility, and a whole series of qualities—human qualities. It requires, fundamentally, that the students be themselves human persons; and indeed as fully human as may be. Not flashes of imagination, necessarily: it may demand long hours, or years, of patient, careful wrestling with the material. And not 'subjective' interpretation, by any means: requisite are careful discipline, cross-checking, the framing of hypotheses and the testing of them against new data, or against personal inquiry, or against the critique of colleagues, and a whole apparatus of critical and self-critical procedures. To be an historian is an art; and, like most arts, it requires skill.

To understand any human behaviour, any human feeling, any human hope or vision, is to recognize that if you had been in that situation, you would have had that particular act or quality or value-judgement as one of your options. Not that you would necessarily have acted as that person did; that would deny human freedom, and indeed one has not understood him or her unless one recognizes that he or she might not have acted that way either, although in the end he or she in fact chose to do so. But to act so would strike you as reasonable in those circumstances; as one of the clearly available, and to some degree cogent, possibilities. You know how it felt to be in that situation, and how it felt to act in that way.

The goal of the historian or other student of human affairs is to reconstruct a given situation in the past or at a distance from oneself with such accuracy that we can know what that situation, factually, was; and with such insight that we can know how it felt to be a human being in that situation. To be an historian of religion is to aim at discovering, objectively, the cumulative tradition of Jews, Hindus, Buddhists, Muslims, and the rest as each actually developed, and at appreciating what it must have been like to be a Jew, or a Hindu, or whatever, at that point in history.

To be an historian, or indeed a rational student in any humane field, is to stand imaginatively in the shoes of others. This is possible, in principle, because we are persons, and because they are persons. Two of the fundamental qualities of humanity are the capacities to understand one another and to be understood.

Not fully, certainly. Yet not negligibly, certainly.

Human beings are that kind of reality, it so happens, that any given two of them—no matter how close together, no matter how far apart, in space, time, culture, temperament—any two of them can arrive at an understanding that is neither 100 per cent nor zero. There is no person on earth that I can fully understand. There is and has been no person on earth that I cannot understand at all.

As I have remarked, my own work has been primarily with the cultural history of the Orient; and the awareness of how objectivist studies of this by Westerners have tended to distort what they have purported to interpret has led me to the new formulation. One does not need, however, to go so far afield. Although studies across cultural boundaries make the matter vivid, yet even intracultural work has begun to recognize some of the same problems, even if a solution has there not yet been found. In 1974, I heard a paper[1] in one of the learned societies' meetings on objectivity in modern sociological thought, where two problems were remarked of the insufficiency of objectivity: one, in its contradistinction from empathy, *Einfühlung, verstehen,* à la Dilthey, and the other, in the fact of the potentially incriminating interdependence of subject and object, or their actual collision.

In the one case were presented the insensitivity and lack of penetration, indeed the distortion, of purely externalist, impersonal 'knowing'. In the other, a growing recognition was noted that the subject-object relationship may itself in certain situations set up a polarity that vitiates, rather than guarantees, understanding. As pointed examples of this were cited the study of the situation of blacks in the United States by white scholars; of the role of women by male scholars; of homosexuality by heterosexual investigators. In these examples what was at issue was the point that the intimate dynamic interaction, in the past and still continuing, between the subject group and the object group in each case is in part constitutive of the situation of the object group—to its discomfort; that the subject group—dominant in each pair, and, in the modern jargon, 'oppressive'—has had a hand in perversely making the object group what it is. This fact inevitably introduces a distortion into such research, it was contended (partly because true knowledge in each case is resisted by the knowers because it would involve a new awareness by them of their own selves).

In the presentation, however, it tended still to be presumed that the deviations from the truth are a function of the fact that pure objectivity is, alas, difficult or impossible to attain. It was argued that candour demands that we recognize the limitations imposed on knowledge by these human or social failings. Yet implicit seemed still the notion that perfect objectivity would be a good thing, if only we could be innocent enough or clever enough to achieve it. I disagree.

I would postulate a law, that what a person does is misunderstood if conceived wholly from the outside.

You will be quick to retort that modern knowledge makes us more aware than ever also of the contrary law: that what a person does is misunderstood if viewed wholly from the inside. Of course! Subjectivism is no royal road to truth, either. Of much that goes into our actions, our feelings, our moral choices, our thinking, we are ignorant; and of what we know, much we distort. We deceive ourselves, as well as others. We delude ourselves, not only outsiders. Objectivity, the externalist approach, was developed to get beyond the inadequacies of individual interiority. That it, too, in its turn is proving inadequate, untrue, less than rational, means that we must go, not back to subjectivity, but forward to a larger vision.

Let us look, then, to those sociological problems that we cited. Ideally, I am suggesting, the goal of research on race relations in the United States is the achievement of an intellectual community comprising at least whites and blacks, and ultimately also third parties, with a corporate self-consciousness, critical and rational, of its own racial condition in this area. The proper aim of those making investigations on this topic is not finally to inform a closed group of scholars, and thus to contribute to the growth of science as a body of objective knowledge in principle outside the lives of those involved; but rather is to provide information, evidence, arguments that will be in principle accessible and persuasive to, designed to be assimilated by, all those involved (and also onlookers from China) and thus to contribute to the construction or promotion of that larger community and to its corporate critical self-consciousness.

The final criterion of the validity of the research, I propose, is its verifiable contribution to such self-consciousness.

This is a very radical suggestion, but is advanced in all seriousness.

Similarly in the status-of-women matter, or regarding homosexuality: not 'they', not 'we', not 'you', but 'some of us' are thus-and-so.

The verification test of any statement about women in society would be whether both men and women, in so far as they are rational, and a body of investigators, in so far as they are methodologically sophisticated, critical, scientific, could all three endorse it. The goal is the corporate critical self-consciousness of a community of persons—and I mean community in the true sense of the word, but at the least intellectual—who can say, and feel, and mean: some of us are men, and some of us are women, and the situation of those among us who are women is such-and-such.

In every aspect of human affairs, we human beings, we persons, may aspire to a corporate critical self-consciousness. In no other way can we truly know.

Another example could well be James Mallory's presidential address in Section II of The Royal Society of Canada in 1974 on cabinet government in Canada.[2] In my analysis of why that was an excellent paper, I would include the facts that the distinguished political scientist who wrote it did so as a critical observer of the cabinet system, as it were from the outside, but at the same time as a participant in the human community of which that system forms a part; and that the paper, although Professor Mallory would doubtless not himself use this phraseology, was in fact calculated to be a contribution to the critical self-consciousness of that particular community.

Moreover, and not quite incidentally, the high quality of the English of that address, and of Professor Mallory's other writings, is surely due in no small part to the tradition inherited from British universities of writing in principle for all rational people, rather than in the growing tradition prevalent in the United States and derived perhaps from Germany of writing in principle for the esoteric group, methodologically segregated, of one's own 'discipline'—though I take it for granted that he aspires to be persuasive to his peers, as well as to both the governors and the governed.

I do not know, however, whether Professor Mallory will countenance my attempt to make explicit in terms of this new theory what he and other humane social scientists have quietly been doing.

With this, we move on to our next issue. I will not pursue further the point that objectivity fails to give true knowledge of what it studies, in the case of human affairs, both in practice and in principle, although this could be developed at very great length, and is enormously important. Rather, I would turn to two other aspects of the problem. One is that in this field objectivity inherently disrupts community; again, both in principle and in practice. The second is that it drastically fails to do justice not only to the known but to the knower; not only to the object of knowledge but to the subject. Knowledge of persons by persons must finally recognize, and affirm, the humanity both of what is studied and of the student. It must rejoice in, and not bemoan, that humanity, in all its depth and richness.

On the first point: community.

It is not only that the new ideal of knowing that I am proposing has, of course, a positive effect towards community, but that the present one has a serious negative effect.

Humane knowledge in my sense postulates community and serves to promote it. My assertion that all knowledge of humans by humans is *ipso facto* self-consciousness is true in so far as all humankind is one. It becomes operative *pari passu* as that unity is seen, is felt, is willed. Otherwise, some may have knowledge of others; and such knowledge can be thought of as external, objective—as has been the case in the recent past. It not only emerges out of separateness, however, but corroborates and furthers it. It serves to disrupt.

One aspect of this is the issue of experimentation. A sub-facet of this that has struck me increasingly of late is the deception practised on persons being studied. A second major issue is that of manipulation, control. Objective knowledge is inherently oriented towards the alienation of persons from each other.

Even at a less gruesome level, there is the issue of prediction. A criterion of objective knowledge, sometimes set forth also as a goal, is the ability to predict. This derives from the natural sciences, and once again illustrates that objective knowledge is appropriate in our dealings with objects. There are certain ways, too complicated to go into here, and with important caveats anyway, in which statistical prediction about groups of people is a function of certain kinds of knowledge. Otherwise, however, the notion of predicting personal behaviour—and I mean, as ever, the predicting by some persons of the behaviour of other persons—though less horrendous than experimenting with them or manipulating them, is still both irrational and inhumane. It is both, in that it denies human freedom. It is an intellectual error, since it postulates what is in fact not true, that men, women and children act mechanically, or quasi-mechanically. It affronts human dignity, since it therein ignores or dismisses one of our most precious, and most characteristic, qualities.

Even at the level of pure theory, objectivity leads to fragmentation; in this case, academic. For there is what seems at first the curious paradox that the concept of objective knowledge leads, when the study is of the human, to knowledge that is in fact subjective. I call this a seeming paradox only, since I still am enough of an old-fashioned rationalist to perceive it as in fact no whit surprising that an intellectual error will presently, when pursued far enough in implementation, end in a self-contradiction. Objective or external knowledge gives us knowledge of objects, of what is external; when the concept is misapplied among ourselves, by giving some an external knowledge of others, it cuts off from community not only those about whom the knowledge is gained, but also those who gain it. The result is a corporate subjectivity on the part of what is in principle a limited group.

Objectivity began as a reaching out towards universalism. What was objectively true was, in principle and by aspiration, to be true for all; explicitly as contrasted with the subjective impressions of private parties. This worked quite well in the natural sciences; that is, for our knowledge of a world that is equally external to all of us. It breaks down, however, when what is involved is a knowledge of some by others. The fallacy, though significant, was somewhat less apparent with intra-cultural studies. We have mentioned as exceptions questions of colour, the sexes, homosexuality, where the problem has been recognized. In general, however, within one's own civilization (including even these instances to some degree), whatever the theory, in fact the knowers, the 'experts', have been participants to some more or less saving degree in the human institution or activity that they studied; or at least have had some more or less surreptitious understanding of it, some more or less effective sympathy with it, and even some sense that their work would be relevant to its members. In cross-cultural studies, on the other hand, and conspicuously sometimes in the studies of alien faith, the objectivity and externality of the knowing have meant quite definitely that the knowledge was designed for, and relevant to, non-participants in the phenomenon, the society, the institution, being analysed.

The academic work of Western scholars in Asia has regularly been clearly and explicitly designed to be read by, and to be of interest to, the closed group of one's 'discipline' back home.

One can argue that this is immoral; but this is not the occasion for that. I could cite some scandalous examples; but I must hurry on. I have argued that it does not render a knowledge that penetrates to the personal level of those studied, which is the most significant level. The third argument, however, and the important one here, is that objective knowledge is idiosyncratic. Just as the early Christian missionary wrote for Christians 'back home', so the sociologist writes for sociologists. And this, not as a foible, like his or her jargon, but on principle. I suggest that there is an intellectual flaw here: one might dub it the 'we/they' fallacy. The thing is amusingly sectarian: one writes only for the boundaried circle of those who share certain presuppositions (and whose ritual is certain methodologies).

This fallacy is enshrined in the contemporary concept of 'discipline', which postulates a particular body of people who esoterically share a certain body of knowledge. It has come to be the case that both in practice and in theory, academics of the objectivist, as distinct from humane, sort read (academically) only within their own discipline, write only for members of their discipline, accept as authoritative criticism the judgement only of those they call their peers, by which they mean other members of their group. And so on. This is subjectivity with a vengeance! Group subjectivity, no doubt; but subjectivity for all that. Objective knowledge of the human leads to subjective knowledge by humans. The importance of this has been little understood, but is major. Its contribution to fragmentation is serious.

Clark Kerr of California formally proclaimed an acquiescence in this multifarious subjectivism when he launched at Harvard the concept of 'multiversity'. That repellent notion is a modern paraphrase of Heraclitus's *idia phronesis*, which the university was developed in order to transcend. The concept of diverse disciplines is a sophisticated and institutionalized version almost of the collapse of the university idea, a failure of rational knowledge. So deeply have most of us become victims of it, however, that criticism of it is hardly either understood or entertained.

The social and human devastation wrought by this disciplinary development has been tragic (almost in the Greek sense: there is a certain nobility in the failure). Human loyalties have therein tended to be transferred from the college or university where one works to the 'professional society' of one's discipline, of which one is a member (with consequent segregation, if not alienation, within the institution, of scholars, from both students and colleagues). The university, with this orientation, tends to be no longer a community of scholars, neither among disciplines, nor between teachers and students. A concept of 'career' has been constructed (so that academic rewards are then conceived in terms of outward status rather than increased vision). The training of graduate students has taken precedence over the educating of undergraduates (the former joining the closed circle of the subjectivism). And so it goes. Despite these social and human ramifications, however, which are woeful, it is the intellectual fallacy involved that concerns me here primarily: the notion that knowledge of the human (of ourselves, after all) is the domain of a multitude of disparate idiosyncrasies.

The recent concept of 'interdisciplinary' is an attempt to construct a ladder by which to climb out of a hole into which genuinely humane studies never fall. One hopes that it is promising. One fears, however, that at best it but enlarges the group of those who know externally (perhaps ideally to the whole behavioural science community), without transcending the subjectivity principle of a closed group, of outside observers.

About this linking of objectivity with the fragmentation of community, however unorthodox the idea, I am very serious. Yet I leave it now to move on to my final section, on the role of the knower in humane knowledge. Just as there is a quality on the part of the persons being studied that escapes purely externalist knowing, so also in the concept of such knowing there is an underappreciation of ourselves as learners. Objectivity inherently misapprehends what happens or should happen to the student or scholar in the process of inquiry.

The notion of objectivity has grown out of work in the natural sciences, where what one investigates—the external world, objects—is seen as less than human, as in some fashion beneath us; where what is known seems legitimately to be subordinated conceptually to the mind that knows. In objective knowledge here, accordingly, there has arisen a stress on method—a concept, drawn from the realm of ends and means, that inherently suggests that what is known is dominated. (I recently heard an academic professional in the field of English literature say in the modern fashion that that field constitutes a body of material to be mastered. One might better think in terms of the student's being mastered by the subject matter, surely!)

Learning in the humanities involves being open to that that may be greater than oneself; greater, at least, than one has been until now. The process of knowing is a process of becoming. It is not a matter of using means, but of assimilating ends. Not *primarily* a matter of using means, certainly; of applying certain methods external to oneself. Methods, so far as they are systematized in formal methodologies, not only are, but are calculated to be, separable from the person who employs them. The point of learning about the natural world is the joy of knowing, and/or the resultant ability to change that world. The point of learning about the human is the joy of knowing, which inherently comprises a changing of oneself.

The concept of methodology, and the stress on method in education, imply that one knows ahead of time what one wants, and has only to find out how to get it. This collides with the principle of humane learning, that one discovers in the course of one's study what one is after, what is worth wanting (what one 'wants' in the old-fashioned literal sense, of what is wanting in one's present stage of becoming). In principle it is possible to learn techniques without ceasing to be basically the kind of person that one was before; to come out of the learning process at heart as one went into it.

The student revolution is relevant here. If a university teaches only techniques, proffers only methods of ascertaining what one already wishes to know, then of course students should decide what they wish to know, and in effect should employ the experts to satisfy these aspirations. They should *use* the university for their own purposes.

Humane learning, however, is not a methodological system for gratifying desires, however worthy. It is an exploration of what we have been, may be, and thereby what we truly, ultimately, are. The individual person who enters upon it is therefore exposing his or her actual self to his or her potential self, is participating in that process of self-transcendence in which being human in part consists.

Humane knowing is an exercise in the meeting between persons, be it across the centuries or across the world. It is, therefore, not technical, subordinate to methodological rules. In personal relations, whether face-to-face or mediated by our symbolic forms of expression, the use of technical procedures, unless rigorously subordinated to primarily personal considerations, is not merely inappropriate but potentially disruptive. Persons cannot know persons except in mutuality; in respect, trust, and equality, if not ultimately love. In this realm of knowing, accordingly, the attitude with which one approaches one's data proves to be at least as significant, as consequential, as the methods with which one handles them. One must be ready not only to receive the other, but to give oneself. In humane knowledge, at stake is one's own humanity, as well as another individual's, or another community's. And at issue is humanity itself.

We have come full circle, then, to my basic thesis: that the new mode for humane knowledge is in terms of a disciplined corporate self-consciousness; critical, comprehensive, global. To study the human is to study oneself—even when one studies another (or one society, another) separated by much space, or time, or both. The corner that we are in process of turning is one the turning of which enables us to see and to feel this; and presently, let us hope, to act in terms of it. We shall act in terms of it because inherent in this kind of knowledge is the further principle that to know something new is to become a new kind of person.

In principle, then, for all humankind to know each other is for all humankind to become one community. And vice-versa: only as we move towards community can we come to know.

This applies to the world the principle on which humanist study has always been based within our own culture. What great individuals have produced makes available to us lesser mortals a vision by which we overcome in part our lessness. There are facets of our common humanity that lie dormant in most of us until awakened by our coming into touch with the attainments of others.

To study a great poem, or a great work of art, or a great idea, is to become more fully human.

And not only what is great can serve us thus. I still hold that there is merit in studying what humans and civilizations have chiefly prized. Yet one can enhance one's vision, one's understanding of oneself, of the human, of the universe, by coming into genuine intellectual apprehension of all, whatever, great or small. We all read what psychiatrists say about their patients. Since those patients are human, as are we, this means: about us.

Our solidarity precedes our particularity; and is part of our self-transcendence. The truth of all of us is part of the truth of each of us.

Several years ago I had occasion to characterize the study of comparative religion as moving from talk of an 'it' to talk of a 'they'; which became a 'we' talking of a 'they'; and presently a 'we' talking of 'you'; then 'we' talking 'with' you; and finally—the goal—'we all' talking together about 'us'. The study of comparative religion is the process, now begun, where we human beings learn, through critical analysis, empirical inquiry, and collaborative discourse, to conceptualize a world in which some of us are Christians, some of us are Muslims, some of us are Hindus, some of us are Jews, some of us are sceptics, some of us are inquirers; and where all of us are, and recognize each other as being, rational people.

One of the most deeply significant facts about any person is who is included when he or she says 'we'. In principle, I am contending, academic intellectuals cannot rest content until they mean 'we human beings', across the globe and across the centuries; and their work must be seen, by them and others, as a contribution towards that. As a beginning, and as a concrete practical step, they must move towards meaning not 'we in my discipline' but 'we persons involved in this particular study: those of us being studied, and those of us studying (in a discipline, if you like, though I should prefer to say, in a university). The truth then that we seek is a truth that can be recognized, assimilated, existentially and critically validated, by both sets of us within this new community'.

Some among you may have felt that I have gone too far, or have been too strident, in my urging our superseding the objectivist orientation. I have come to feel strongly on the matter through awareness of the pain and resentment on the part of Asians before the aggression of much Western academic scholarship. More recently and nearer home, I have become alert to the growing resentment of students in Western society before modern academic study's aggression against the person.

The established doctrine and the, to some, seemingly ritualized procedure of the current phase of the modern scientific movement seem massively solid, not easily opened to critical revision. As a historian of religion, I am familiar with the difficulty, intellectual and emotional, that the carriers of a system have when their orthodoxy is challenged, the basic postulates of their tradition questioned. If some of you, as carriers of scientific orthodoxy, resist my heresy; if you find bizarre my intellectualist thesis that there is something starkly and profoundly awry with the impersonalism of modern orientation to knowledge; at least you must find sobering the practical, and by implication also theoretical, challenge posed by student dissidence. Universities that have succumbed to the recent mis-orientation, as I call it, are subject to that otherwise enigmatic wonder, of appearing repellent to the sensitive. I hope that no one in this audience underestimates the deep significance of the alienation from the university of many of our most intelligent, sensitive, youth.

And indeed this matters outside the university too, in Western society at large. Although this is not my subject, yet one may at least in passing remark that as our culture has become increasingly permeated with what passes for a scientific outlook on knowledge and the world, and also on human matters, the increasing success in dealing with things has been accompanied, as everyone knows, with an increasing sickness of personal and social life: the depersonalization of social procedures, the fragmentation of community, the alienation of persons from their neighbour, from themselves, and from the world. As a humanist, I resist blaming this on science; I blame it on objectivization, misapplied from natural science to thinking about human affairs. And I certainly resist the notion, championed by many imitative scientistic spokesmen, that the only alternative to objectivity is subjectivism—a fallacy so loudly proclaimed that some believe it and therefore, fleeing from depersonalizing objectivity, turn to irrationality or even to drugs.

Impersonalism in human affairs is, I argue, bad science, is irrational; and the alternative to both objectivity, which is false, and subjectivity, which is radically inadequate, is a rational personalism in community.

But enough.

I began by speaking of the humane sciences, which concern the human, and the human sciences, which all sciences are. I close by returning to that starting point. That science as such, natural and other, be thought of as human, not absolute, is itself important. I have insisted on the deep differences between our knowledge of the material world and our knowledge of ourselves. Yet I believe in the unity of knowledge, as I believe in the unity of humankind. I do not wish to disrupt the former. Although again outside my own field of competence, I think it perhaps not absurd to suggest that the concept of corporate human self-consciousness, which I have propounded, could subsume, in the end, the natural and the life sciences, without infringing their integrity. I am passionate, as you see, in insisting that to subordinate our study of humankind to the categories of our study of the objective world is irrational as well as inhumane, and potentially destructive. Yet we can avoid bifurcating knowledge, at the theoretical level, by recognizing that our study of the objective world, science as a human enterprise, may quite legitimately be envisaged as a corporate critical consciousness on the part of humankind of the material world in which we live as it appears objectively to us humans, and not detachedly as absolute knowledge of that world as it is in and of itself.

Given the ecological crisis, the atomic bomb, and the moral implications of modern genetics, to understand all science responsibly as ideally a form of critical human consciousness seems not perhaps unreasonable.

However that may be, that we must learn to see our knowledge of ourselves in this light, under pain of both error and disaster, is my primary submission.

NOTES

CHAPTER 3. PHILOSOPHIA AS ONE OF THE
RELIGIOUS TRADITIONS OF HUMANKIND

1. See, for example: 'Conversion to Philosophy', being chapter XI of A.D. Nock, *Conversion: The Old and the New in Religion from Alexander the Great to Augustine of Hippo*; A.J. Festugière, *Épicure et ses dieux*; Werner Jaeger, 'Über Ursprung und Kreislauf des philosophischen Lebensideals'; an English translation of this was published as an appendix to the second edition of this author's *Aristotle: Fundamentals of the History of his Development*, pp. [426]–461, as 'On the Origin and Cycle of the Philosophic Ideal of Life'; and Werner Jaeger, *Humanism and Theology*.

2. See Werner Cohn, 'What is Religion? An Analysis for Cross-Cultural Comparisions', *Journal of Christian Education*, 1964, 7, [116]–138; Id., '"Religion", in Non-Western Countries', *American Anthropologist*, 1967, 69, 73–76; and Id., 'On the Problem of Religion in Non-Western Cultures', in *Internationales Jahrbuch für Religionssociologie/International Yearbook for the Sociology of Religion*, 1969, 5, [7]–19.

3. See the recent elaborate study of Michel Despland, *La Religion en Occident: évolution des idées et du vécu*, which followed the earlier brief treatment in chapter 2, '"Religion" in the West', in my *The Meaning and End of Religion*.

4. As translated by Arthur Waley in his *Three Ways of Thought in Ancient China*, 79.

5. Cf. the references in our note 2 *supra*.

6. On the novelty of this 19th-century notion that believing is what religious people primarily do, see my *Belief and History*; and 'The English Word "Believe"', being chapter 6 of my *Faith and Belief*.

7. Wilfred Cantwell Smith, *Towards a World Theology: Faith and the Comparative History of Religion*, 154ff.

8. E.g., W.E. Soothill (London and New York, [1913, 1923] 1929).

9. Mrs. Annie Besant. She apparently persuaded at least herself, and perhaps some Hindu priest, to believe that she had been Hindu in previous incarnations.

10. This passage first appeared in my 'Traditional Religion and Modern Culture', 68–69; and was introduced again in slightly modified wording in 'Religion as Symbolism', reprinted above as Chapter 1. The present citation merges the two wordings slightly, with slightly modified punctuation.

11. It serves as, for instance, the title of a book by Martin Foss (Princeton: Princeton University Press, 1946)—a book that sets out to criticize and in the end to reject the idea.

12. It seems probable, although not certain, that it was in this latter sense that Protagoras himself first uttered the maxim. Scholarly discussion of this point is conveniently summarized in a careful discussion in W.K.C. Guthrie, *A History of Greek Philosophy*, vol. III, 188–192.

13. One thinks, for example, of Auguste Comte's religion of humanity with its personification of humanity in the female figure (with child in arms) of Clotilde de Vaux. See, for example, the frontispiece of the *Catéchisme Positiviste*, of Auguste Comte, published by the Apostolat Positiviste du Brésil, Rio de Janerio: Temple of Humanité, 1957, reproducing the frontispiece from the Parisian edition of Jorge Lagarrigue ('Apôtre de l'Humanité') of 1891.

14. The statement as such does not seem to be found in Greek. One approximation is Chrysippus, as quoted in Plutarch, *De Virtute Morali*, 450D (e.g., page 72 of vol. 6, 1939, in the edition, with English translation, of W.C. Helmbold, *Plutarch's Moralia*, 14 vol., Cambridge, Mass.: Harvard University Press, and London: Heinemann).

15. *Stromata*, Book 1, chap. 5, section 28: 2, 3. An English translation reads as follows: 'God is responsible for all good things: of some, like the blessings of the old and new covenants, directly; of others, like the riches of philosophy, indirectly. Perhaps philosophy too was a direct gift of God to the Greeks before the Lord extended his appeal to the Greeks. For philosophy was to the Greek world what the Law was to the Hebrews, a tutor escorting them to Christ. So philosophy is a preparatory process; it opens the road for the person whom Christ brings to his final goal.' Clement of Alexandria, *Stromateis Books One to Three*, tr. John Ferguson, *The Fathers of the Church: A new Translation*, Vol. 85 (Washington D.C.: The Catholic University of America Press, 1991) 42. The original version of this article cited the *Sources chrétiennes* edition of the Greek:

Clement D'Alexandrie, *Les Stromates*, Stromate I (Claude Mondésert, introd.; Marcel Caster, trad. et notes. Paris: Editions du Cerf, 1951), 65.

16. Friedrich Schleiermacher, *Der christliche Glaube*, 2nd ed., I. iii. 12, § 3. In the English trans. p. 62: 'If the Mosaic Law belongs to the one chain of this divine economy of salvation, then we must, according to approved Christian teachers, include also the Greek philosophy, especially that which tended towards Monotheism.' Schleiermacher then also refers to Clement, although to a different passage from the one that I have just cited. He makes the reservation that heathen philosophy must not be thought of as forming a single whole with Christianity; but this same reservation applies for him to Judaism.

CHAPTER 4.   ON MISTRANSLATED BOOKTITLES

1. José Ortega y Gasset, posthumously, in *Diogenes*, number 28, 1959. This UNESCO review appeared simultaneously in four languages: English, French, German, and Spanish. In this particular case, the original was presumably the Spanish version, but despite extensive search this has not proven available in North America. In English: 'The Difficulty of Reading' (Clarence E. Parmenter, trans.), 1–17 of the English issue.

2. In addition to the works considered here, I have on occasion elsewhere treated other illustrative instances where current Western presuppositions are erroneously read into perceptions of earlier positions in the religious realm, and the error represented in the received English titles of quite pivotal works. For misleading but standard wordings for Augustine's *De Trinitate* ('On the Trinity' is misleading, or at least anachronistic), for Calvin's *Christianae Religionis Institutio* ('The Institutes of the Christian Religion') is surely wrong), and for Augustine's and Zwingli's *De Vera [. . .] Religione* (originally, not concerned with 'the true religion'), see the observations in my *Belief and History*, pp. 122–123, and my *The Meaning and End of Religion*, pp. 35–37, 28–31 and again 35–37, respectively.

3. Émile Durkheim. The first edition, bearing this title and with the subtitle *Le système totémique en Australie*, was published in Paris: Felix Arcan, 1912, in the series *Bibliothèque de philosophie contemporaine*. The English translation by Joseph Ward Swain, *The Elementary Forms of the Religious Life: a study in religious sociology*, London: Allen & Unwin, and New York: Macmillan, no date, appeared in 1915. Both French and English have been several times reprinted since, recent editions being by other publishers in both cases.

4. In both tendencies Durkheim was a full and indeed leading participant. On the former point, he is quite explicit. He defends the view that 'the primitive religions . . . can . . . serve to show the nature of the religious life' (Fr., p. 4; Eng., p. 3)—that is, in its essentials. While agreeing that 'the most recent religions' (*ibid*)—which are admittedly of a 'greater complexity and [a] higher ideology' (Fr., p. 3; Eng., p. 3)—might in principle be thought to serve equally well, he characterizes them as in practice so remote from their origins [*sic*] and so complicated, so transformed by later obscuring interpretations, that in their case 'it is very difficult to distinguish . . . the essential [*sic*] from the accessory' (Fr., p. 7; Eng., p.5). Referring to 'the mark of its origins' (sc., the origins of 'the religious fact') and, therefore, to its/their 'true nature', he writes: 'it would have been well-nigh impossible to infer them from the study of the more developed religions' (Fr., p. 10; Eng., pp. 7–8).

The second point, that present-day 'primitive' societies and their religions and other institutions are primitive in a chronological sense, in being not unlike all human society in its historically earliest forms, Durkheim like others of his time took on the whole for granted. He noticed the problem in passing but dismissed it (cf. Fr., p. 1n, and p. 11; Eng., p. 1n., and p. 8). They did not wrestle with the fact that modern 'primitives' have just as many years of history behind them as do the rest of us to-day.

Both matters, as well as the notion of elements as constitutive, universal, and on-going, are made clear in his opening chapter, 'Introduction', are evident throughout, and are addressed again in his final chapter, 'Conclusion'.

Both were representative of the then prevalent ideology among intellectuals (and both crystallized in the term *élémentaire*) which viewed 'knowledge as the reduction of complex wholes to simple elements' (Wm. Sullivan), and rejected final causes.

5. I have used the following edition: *S. Thomae Aquinatis doctoris angelici Liber de Veritate Catholicae Fidei contra errores Infidelium, qui dicitur Summa Contra Gentiles*, ed. Cesla[us] Pera, D. Petr[us] Marc, et al., Augustae Taurinorum: Marietti, 3 vol., 1961–7. (The title-pages of vol. 2 and 3, which were published first, vary slightly in wording.)

6. St. Thomas Aquinas, *On the Truth of the Catholic Faith: Summa Contra Gentiles, translated, with an Introduction and Notes,* by Anton C. Pegis et al., Garden City, New York: Doubleday (Image Books), 5 vol., 1955–7. (There is occasion just below—in our next note—to refer to an impressive version earlier in the century: Joseph Rickaby, S.J., *Of God and His Creatures: an annotated translation (with some abridgement) of the Summa contra Gentiles of Saint Thos Aquinas*, St. Louis: Herder, and London: Burns & Oates, MCMV.)

7. *S. Thomae Aquinatis . . . Quaestiones Disputatae*, vol. I: *De Veritate*, ed. Raymund[us] Spiazzi, Taurini, Romae: Marietti, 1964. So far as I am aware, recent English versions of this always render it as 'on truth', never 'on reality': an example, St. Thomas Aquinas, *Truth*, James B. McGlynn, trans., Chicago: Henry Regner, 3 vol., 1952–4. How would those who might balk at rendering the word here as 'reality' respond to a suggestion of calling in both: *On Truth and Reality?* The problem stems from what 'truth' means to most academic intellectuals in the late twentieth century. (I find engaging the title and Preface [pp. vii–viii] of the Rickaby translation of Thomas's other work cited in our immediately preceding note just above.)

8. In *Belief and History* and *Faith and Belief*. (Cf. also my *Meaning and End of Religion*, not least the material summarized on its p. 77.)

9. Thomas Aquinas, *Utrum fides sit una*. In his *Summa Theologiae*, 2: 2: 4: 6. In the Caramello edn., Turin and Rome: Marietti, Vol. 2, 32.

10. Let not this sentence seem to suggest that Raymond was more appreciative than was Thomas of the Muslims and their religious life; far from it. He is known as a zealous supporter of the Inquisition, and of a crusade (1299) against 'the Moors'. He was simply more appreciative than was Thomas of the fact of the Muslims' existence: a fact that otherwise hardly impinged on Thomas's consciousness, who of course also knew nothing of Hindus, Buddhists, and China. It was at Raymond's instigation that Thomas took time off to write *contra Gentiles* at all; the question would not have occurred to him on his own.

11. He does indeed occasionally use that phrase in his writings; yet if I may quote from a recent observation: 'In my *Belief and History* . . . I made the following statement: "in Catholic thought, it is my impression that throughout the Middle Ages the dominant custom was for the concept *fides* to be used without specification". . . . Through the sumptuous new computerized concordance it is now possible to specify this more precisely. In the Thomas corpus the ratio of *fides* alone to *fides christiana* (or *christiana fides*) is 132 to 1.' This is from my *Faith and Belief*, 299, where supporting references will be found for the data used in the statistical calculation.

12. Cf. my *Meaning and End of Religion*, p. 227, n. 87, for Zwingli's *De religione christiana* as having signified, in its time, 'the piety that Christ has made available'.

13. More explicitly: 'false faith' for him is a contradiction in terms:

> *ei [sc, fides] non potest subesse falsum.*
> *. . . fidei non potest subesse aliquod falsum.*
> *. . . prout cadit sub fide, non potest esse falsum.*

(*Summa Theologiae*, 2: 2: I: 3—in the Caramello edition, vol. 2, 5–6). Furthermore, for him faith differs from all intellectual activities that have to do with the true-false alternative: *distinguitur iste actus qui est credere ab omnibus actibus intellectus qui sunt circa verum vel falsum*—ibid., 2: 2: 2: I (Caramello, vol. 2, 16).

14. Generic nouns in English may be preceded by a definite article when followed at once by a qualifying clause or epithet (examples: 'the courage that she showed', 'the piety of those Muslims').

15. *Faith and Belief*, 297–9

16. *propositum nostrae intentionis est veritatem quam fides catholicae profitetur . . . manifestare*: book I, chap. 2; in the Pera edn. (n. 5, above), vol. 2, page 3, §9. The matter is elaborated and richly corroborated in the subsequent few introductory chapters. Cf. also our next note just below.

17. See for example chapters 6–9 of Book I; esp. chap. 7. There is a further point: that one could—of course—contend that to translate *ratio* by 'reason' here is itself a betrayal, given the gulf between the Latin term's thirteenth-century resonance, cosmic as well as human, and the much reduced meaning that the English one has for most twentieth-century academics, and indeed modern culture generally. See, for instance, G.-Ed. Demers, 'Les divers sens du mot "ratio" au moyen âge'.

18. Friedrich Schleiermacher, *Der christliche Glaube: nach den Grundsätzen der evangelischen Kirche im Zusammenhange dargestellt*, 1830 (and many times reprinted. I have used the Martin Redeker edition, Berlin: de Gruyter, 2 vol., 1960).

19. Friedrich Schleiermacher, *The Christian Faith*, English Translation of the Second German Edition, H.R. Mackintosh and J.S. Stewart, ed., 1928 (and many times reprinted). The translation 'has been executed by various hands' (vi): the Introduction, with which we are here primarily concerned, by D.B. Baillie, but other parts by W.R. Matthews, Edith Sandbach-Marshall, A.B. Macauley, Alexander Grieve, J.Y. Campbell, and the two editors; Professor Mackintosh having 'exercised a general supervision over the work as a whole' (ibid.).

20. *Über die Religion: Reden an die Gebildeten unter ihren Verächtern*, (1799). There was a second edition, with significant modifications, Berlin: Reimer, 1806; and a final third edition substantially unchanged from the second except for the addition of short *Erläuterungen* at the end of each of the five Speeches. The English translation by Oman (see our n. 22 below) is of the third edn., but discusses the differences among the three with some care. The tendency to specify religion as a generic something

was crystallizing in Germany at this time. In a title it had been adumbrated five years earlier in Kant, *Die Religion innerhalb der Grenzen der blossen Vernunft*; and was carried forward by Hegel. On this development in general see chapter 2, '"Religion" in the West' of my *Meaning and End* . . . , and esp. its §vii, 44–8; and a later more elaborate study of the matter in Michel Despland, *La Religion en occident*. Schleiermacher comments in passing on the newness of the term, in his *Der christliche Glaube*, §6: 47/31.

(Note: here and elsewhere in what follows, I observe the usual custom of citing a passage of this work by giving its section or paragraph number; then, after a colon, my references separated by a virgule indicate the page number of the Redeker edition 1960 (n. 18, above) of the German, followed by the page number of the English. Unless otherwise specified, the German page number refers to the first volume, from which virtually all our citations here are taken. This order, giving preference to the original German, with the English translation following, is maintained in all cases, even when the English is presented first in our text.)

21. The issue here is that members of a new movement, seeing the world in a new way, think of other or older ways of seeing it as particular (peculiar), limited, and to some degree at least, wrong; that their own way of seeing it is also particular, limited, and to some degree at least inadequate they themselves are hardly the ones to articulate. To them it is *the* way, not a way. The modern West's secular ideology which conceptualizes religion as an addendum to the human and to society or culture has even yet hardly been widely recognized as idiosyncratic, by being given a prevalent and self-accepted name. Even the concept 'secularism' was launched some decades after Schleiermacher. (The silly term 'postmodern' is a move in this direction made nowadays by grouping themselves as (cohesively?) outside what it sees as a coalesced ideology which it is rejecting and superseding; deeming both 'modern' and 'post-modern' to be then not descriptive adjectives with the individual terms' normal meaning (the latter compound is, strictly, inherently meaningless), but proper names, disparaging and laudatory respectively. Recently a philosopher, who shall be nameless, has compounded the amusing confusion by propounding, in a title, the charming phrase 'beyond the post-modern . . .'.)

The terms 'Christian', 'Hindu', 'Buddhist', 'Mohammedan', 'Quaker', 'Wahhabi', 'Confucian', and many another are instances of originally external naming. (Muslims have been relatively successful in recent decades in resisting the 'Mohammedan' name by substituting an honorific Arabic term—Islam—whose meaning the West did not understand, and therefore has hesitated about only out of inertia.)

22. Friedrich Schleiermacher, *On Religion: speeches to its cultured despisers. Translated, with introduction,* by John Oman. London: Kegan Paul, Trench, Trübner, 1893. (Several times reprinted; also in abridged editions, e.g., by E. Graham Waring.)

23. This was greatly developed presently; later in the century, books and articles with this specific title, generic singular and particularist plural, appear. This question, too, goes back to Kant; he does not seem to use the plural *Religionen,* but does call it a 'practical religious illusion' (*Religion innerhalb* . . . p. 255) to confuse what he calls *Religion* with the historical organized institutions; each of these he tends to call a *statutarische Religion* or *Pfaffentum.* Schleiermacher, also, addresses the issue in the *Reden:* Speech Five is entitled *Die Religionen/*'The Religions'. For him, these are various outward manifestations (*Erscheinungen*—e.g., p. 360 of the 3rd edn.; Oman, p. 214) of, providing opportunity for, the real thing, the generic; *in den Religionen sollt Ihr die Religion entdecken* (p. 355; 'I would have you discover religion in the religions'—p. 211).

It may be noted that during the course of the twentieth century both German and, a little later, French, evinced a minor tendency to move—to a quite limited degree—towards the English custom, of dispensing with an article altogether, for both generic and indefinite. One example: D. Otto Pfleiderer, *Religion und Religionen,* München: J.F. Lehmann, 1906.

24. See my *Towards a World Theology.*

25. I have used the recent edition in *Petri Abaelardi Opera Theologica,* where his *Theologia Christiana* is volume II (Corpus Christianorum, Continuatio mediaeualis, no. 12), ed. Eligius M. Buytaert (Turnholti: Brepols, 1969), 5–372. There is an English analysis in J. Ransom McCallum, *Abelard's Christian Theology,* Oxford: Basil Blackwell, 1948.

26. The polarity has been set forth especially in German, where *der christliche Glaube und die nichtchristlichen Religionen* or the like (e.g., in various titles) might almost be thought standard. Sometimes one finds *das Evangelium* or *die Botschaft* in place of *der christliche Glaube* in the contrast; *Botschaft* representing the Greek *kerygma.* (The title of Hendrik Kraemer's influential work, *The Christian Message in a Non-Christian World* [London: Edinburgh House, 1938], was much flatter in English than it would be in German.) In English, the Christian complex is more likely to be called also a religion, or the others more likely to be called faiths (World Council of Churches publications, for example, and various titles; although even so liberal a thinker as A.C. Bouquet adopts the other pattern: cf. his *The Christian Faith and non-Christian Religions,* [London:] Nisbet and New York: Harper, 1958.)

In pluralism as such, Barth himself was not interested. The term would have seemed to him far too drastic a concession: he acknowledged a plurality of religions, but never became aware of plurality of forms of, incidence of, faith. The issue is one to which nothing impinged on his attention in such a way as to induce him to pay heed. Some among his followers more caught up in to-day's global situation, however, adopted his concepts and categories. (Their books and articles use *Botschaft* and *Evangelium*, as well as *Glaube*, in setting Christians' involvement in sharp contrast with other communities' *Religionen*.)

A polarity between faith, or the relation to God that Christians are vouchsafed, and religion, is developed systematically by Barth in his *Kirchliche Dogmatik* (see esp. vol. I, Part 2, §17); but is adumbrated already in 1921 in his *Römerbrief*, where he resorts to the term *Religion* sparingly but when he does so presenting it as something historical (in almost every instance some form of the word *Geschichte* appears on the same line or even in the same compound or anyway nearby) and evidently therefore as merely (*sic*) human, in his almost pejorative sense. Later, his attack on it is direct and a whit explosive.

In the course of my work preparing this present study a new hypothesis was generated in my mind as seemingly a contribution to making coherent sense of quite a considerable array of data. It involves a refinement on my study of several years ago (in my *Meaning and End* . . .) of the ambiguous development in Western civilization, over the centuries, of the concept 'religion'—an ambiguity that prompted that study's proposal to discriminate intellectually between what it calls 'cumulative tradition', and faith. Confusing the two can prove serious, doubly so when diverse traditions (including other peoples' or other centuries' ununderstood traditions) are involved. The new hypothesis suggests and would explain a further discrimination: between the use historically of the Latin word *religio* and its cognates in other modern European languages, on the one hand, and in German, on the other, to name one, or the other, or both (or now one, now the other) of these two intersecting dimensions of humankind's religious life. The task would be to ascertain and to scrutinize how the term has been used in respectively the two cases. I have not yet tested the hypothesis rigorously; but in a preliminary way have come upon many supporting data, and a few predictions based on it have been borne out. It clarifies, too, the 'others have religion, we have faith', which has seemed reasonable to many more Germans than, so rendered, to anglophones.

It would help to make more understandable both Barth's above section on *Religion* (and his and his school's position on the matter generally), and the impression of startling uncouthness made by its English version ('The Abolition of Religion', 'Religion as Unbelief', and so on), plus a number of other matters that appear to be illuminated by it. (Cf. 'religionless Christianity'.) It helps to corroborate also and to clarify our general thesis here that translating may make visible serious differences in the presuppositions and world-views of divergent cultures or ages.

The suggestion is that there tends to be a significant difference between the meaning of *Religion* in German, and 'religion' in English and the Romance languages (—even to the point where at times a straight translation may inescapably be misleading) because of the Latinate term's having come into German a thousand years later (cf. end of the penultimate para. of n. 20 above).

27. See especially my *Belief and History* and *Faith and Belief*, and one might mention also my *Towards a World Theology*.

28. *Der christliche Glaube*, §8:57/38. The entire *Zusatz*/Postscript 1, from which our quotation here is taken, and indeed the entire section (§8) to which it is attached (51ff./34ff.), are highly pertinent; it is they to which the first part of our sentence in the text refers.

29. *Von den Verschiedenheiten der frommen Gemeinschaften überhaupt*/'The Diversities of Religious Communions in General' (§§7–10:47–74/31–52). See esp §7 and, as in our preceding note just above, §8 (pp. 47–58/31–9).

30. To give one illustrative example, on p. 483 of the English, the word generically is used as a running title, and in addition it occurs so eight times on the page (never with an article). (The corresponding German passage, volume 2, 155–6, of course uses the definite article throughout, as the generic demands.) (This page was chosen not altogether at random: rather, it is the only reference in the English index to faith, outside the Introduction, yet specifically to faith 'in Jesus', so that particularity would be more probable here than on average.) I have checked other pages somewhat at random, and find the same pattern. I cannot vouch beyond a limited degree for the impression that outside the Introduction the expression 'the faith' as a translation of *der Glaube* does not occur in the book. Of course, the matter is complicated by the fact that the translation has been 'executed by various hands'. Yet I have checked sample pages from a part rendered by each of the seven translators. I find one instance (§137: English, p. 633) where the word 'faith' occurs generically, without an article, twice, but also once with the article, in the construction where it is followed by a descriptive characterization: 'the faith evoked in the candidate for baptism'/*von dem in dem Taufkandidaten bewirkten Glauben* (volume 2, p. 335)—where in English it could be dubbed ambiguous whether it be generic or particular: as we have remarked

(note 14, above), the one instance where the generic suffers an article is in a construction of this kind, just as, on this same page in the English, the translators write, 'God is not a God of disorder', not 'God is not a god of disorder' with the lower-case initial for the latter. The article in this particular syntactical pattern does not make it into a common noun, as otherwise 'a god' does. (Even in the baptism case here, it may be noted, the particular faith is not 'the Christian faith' as one of the faiths of the world, distinct from the Jewish or Islamic or Hindu, but the faith of one particular Christian person, as distinct from that of his Christian brother.)

My spot-checking has unearthed, for instance, 'the Christian faith' which proves to be a rendering once again (sc., as in the Introduction—cf. the parenthesis two sentences further on, and the next paragraph, in my text) of *die christliche Glaubensweise* (§32:172/132); and *der christliche Glaube*, which comes out as 'that Christian belief which . . .' (§32:172/131); *der wahre Glaube*, rendered as 'true faith' (§109:II,172/496); and so on.

31. By 'Introduction' I designate §§1–31:[8]–167/3–128. (There is a brief subsection at the beginning of this, also called *Einleitung*/'Introduction', three pages in German, two in English: §1:[8]–10/1–2). This, and esp. its long First Chapter (§§2–19:10–125/3–93), is the one part of the book where Christian particularity is set in the context of faith in general throughout history and the world, where the plural context of Christian faith is addressed, and where one might suppose that, if anywhere, particularizing wording would occur. Thus, if there were an occasion for him to use a plural such as 'faiths', it would presumably be here. And indeed, this seems to be the case for the English. This is the one part of the book where my scrutiny of the wording, and collation of the translation with the original, have been more or less thorough; cf. the preceding note.

32. §12:84/61. The one other occasion where this phrase occurs in the Introduction (§3:18/7), they render it as 'Christian belief'—not 'the Christian belief'—in a passage where it is parallel to *die christliche Frömmigkeit* and *das christliche Tun* ('Christian piety . . . Christian belief . . . and Christian action', each without the article in English). We may note also that *der Glaube an Christum* appears as 'belief in Christ' (§10:66/46, tris) and *der Glaube an Jesum* as 'faith in Jesus' (§14:94/68); though *der Glaube an* einen *Gott* as 'the [*sic*] belief in one God' (§10:66/46). In note 30 above attention was called to the use once again later in the book of the phrase *der christliche Glaube*, rendered as 'that Christian belief which . . .'.

33. The observations of nn. 30 and 32 above apply equally here, so far as completeness of scrutiny is concerned.

34. (Wording such as 'the piety' or 'pieties', or 'the Christian piety', would indeed be strained, would even for twentieth-century thought constitute uncouth English.) 'Christian piety'—*die christliche Frömmigkeit* (§3:18/7—cf. our n. 31—and Part IV title, immediately preceding §15:105/76). 'Forms of piety': see our n. 36 below.

35. §10:67/46. Cf. '(the two) other monotheistic faiths' for (*die beiden*) *andern monotheistischen Glaubensweisen*, §9:63/43, §10:67/46. Further, 'all developed faiths', *jede ausgebildete Glaubensweise*, §10:64/44; 'other such faiths', *von andern solchen*, §11:74/52. It should also be noted that this wording was followed a century later by Martin Buber, who chose this form for a plural for his striking work *Zwei Glaubensweisen*, Zürich: Manese, 1950—perhaps the first genuine study ever of more than one 'mode' of faith, taking each seriously and considering them comparatively. Noteworthy too is that the English version of this a year later chose a rather more rigid term: *Two Types of Faith*, Norman P. Goldhawk, trans., London: Routledge & Kegan Paul, and New York: Macmillan, 1951. Cf. also our next note.

36. §11:74/52; §10:68/47. On the former, cf. our note 35 just above. On the latter, cf. '(not . . .) a distinctive way of faith'—(*keine*) *eigene Glaubensweise*; 'each faith'—*jede Glaubensweise*, 'one faith'—*eine Glaubensweise* (all three: §10:67/46); 'any particular faith'—*eine einzelne Glaubensweise*, again (§11:75/52). We have already seen that 'the faith' is *die Glaubensweise* (§10:68/47). Cf. also below, at n. 38.

37. §7:48/32. More fully: *es gibt . . . Gestaltungen gemeinsamer Frömmigkeit*. As indicated, however, this is unusual; regularly, this phrase emerges rather as 'forms of piety': §7:50/33, §8:51/34, §9:59/39, §9:60/41. Also: *Gattungen der Frömmigkeit*, 'kinds of piety' (§7:50/35). Cf. also above, at n. 33.

38. §7:50/33. The phrase occurs twice more in the Introduction, but in both cases comes out as 'Christian piety'—see n. 34 above. Sometimes (and on this, one might reflectively compare n. 26 above) the noun without the qualifying adjective (*christliche*) is rendered as 'religion' without an article: *die Frömmigkeit* becomes simply 'religion' (§3:15/6)—occasionally with the alternative explicit: 'religion or piety' (§3:15/5). *Eine . . . Richtung der Frömmigkeit* appears as 'a type of religion' (§11:74/52); *Gestalt der Frömmigkeit*, 'form of religion' (§8:55/37).

39. §10:68/47.

40. See above, at nn. 28, 29. He is quite explicit about lower and higher, and fairly so about 'forms'; using for instance, such a phrase as *eine*

höhere Religionsform (§7:48/32; and cf. our next note just below). On the next page, however, 'forms of faith' is once again *Glaubensweisen*. 'The purest form of Monotheism' is *die reinste . . . Gestaltung des Monotheismus* (§8:56/38).

41. . . . *das Christentum in der Tat die vollkommenste unter den am meisten entwickelten Religionsformen ist/'*. . . Christianity is, in fact, the most perfect of the most highly developed forms of religion' (§8:56/38). See in general Part II of that First Chapter (cf. n. 29 above). (Rendering the 'most' developed here as 'the most highly developed' is presumably legitimate enough, since the author has indeed set forth an historically progressivist thesis, equating lower with earlier and higher with later— except that Christianity is higher than Islam.)

42. . . . *mit der bei jedem Christen vorauszusetzenden Überzeugung von der ausschliessenden Vortrefflichkeit des Christentums/'*. . . the conviction, which we assume every Christian to possess, of the exclusive superiority of Christianity' (§7:50/33).

CHAPTER 5. SHALL NEXT CENTURY BE SECULAR OR RELIGIOUS?

1. In 1903 was published F.S.C. Schiller, *Humanism: philosophical essays* (London: Macmillan). Some of its chapters had no doubt appeared earlier in learned journals; in book form the author averred that he hoped that his views would reach 'the general public' (opening page of the 'Preface'), which indeed they did. The Preface makes quite clear that he was consciously giving the term 'humanism' a new meaning. He notes that earlier he had attempted to use 'anthropomorphism' in this new sense, but had decided that altering the prevalent meaning of that term 'may prove difficult'; he had higher hopes for his proposed new use of the other term—hopes that turned out to be validated by events. 'I propose . . . to convert to the use of philosophic terminology a word which has long been famed in history and literature, and to denominate HUMANISM the attitude of thought which . . . is destined, I believe, to win the widest popularity.' (Preface to the first edition; I have used the second, 1912, edn., where this passage is reproduced on pp. xix–xx.) Again, he speaks of the 'transfer of its (sc., this term's) old associations to a novel context' (ibid., p. xxv of the 2nd edn.); and he devotes space to defending this new use of the term. In his Preface to the Second Edition almost a decade later (ibid., p. ix), he notes that his 'choice of the word "Humanism" as expressive of' the novel outlook 'has been vindicated'. Writing as a philosopher (that is, within the Graeco-Roman stream in civilization),

his explicit thesis is that the new view being advocated is proffered as an alternative not to theism, which he is inclined to set aside, so much as to Platonism and all that it has involved—the chief other grounding, apart from the Judaeo-Christian, in Western history of the transcendentalist outlook. (Nonetheless, he retains 'idealism' and even the concept of life after death.) Also, in the following year, 1904, William James was reporting his having been speculating as to whether this same term was likely 'to succeed in the struggle to gain currency'—thinking this probably unlikely in philosophic circles at least, but saying that it does indeed express 'the essence of the new way of thought. . . .'—see s.v. HUMANISM in the revised Oxford English Dictionary, §5. 'Philos.'; see also §3, ibid., for 19th century uses.

2. See Wilfred Cantwell Smith, *Belief and History*, and *Faith and Belief*.

CHAPTER 7. A HUMAN VIEW OF TRUTH

1. On the matter of the classical Islamic view of the morality of truth and lies, it is perhaps not inappropriate to quote here something that I had occasion to write elsewhere in commenting on a work of Muhammad ibn 'Abd al-Karīm al-Shahrastānī (1076–1153) who, in a particular passage, 'contends that a false sentence is not intrinsically better or worse, morally, than a true one. Some truths, he says, are not very pretty. (Keats was inspired by an urn to remind us that this view is un-Grecian.) There are some who would agree with this, holding that it is not lies themselves, but the telling of lies, that is wrong. Our author goes further: for him, the telling of lies, even, is not intrinsically moral or immoral. What is wrong, hellishly so, is for *me* to tell a lie—or for you to do so. And the reason for this is that God has created us and has commanded us not to lie.' In George A. Makdisi (ed.) *Arabic and Islamic Studies in Honor of Hamilton A.R. Gibb* (Leiden: Brill 1965), 598.

2. And what eternity is all about, too, in a sense. The reality of the objective world, although it is prior to our personal orientation to that reality, in the end will vanish while the way that you and I have responded to that reality is of a transcending significance which, to use the poetic imagery, will survive, will cosmically outlast the world. The mundane world is independent of us humans and is not to be subordinated to our whims. Yet ultimately, in this vision, a human if she or he relates herself or himself truly to reality is greater than the world.

3. I say 'trilateral' because in the case of, for instance, a statement three matters are involved: the person who makes the statement, the statement itself, and the facts that it purports to describe. (In a game, cheating sim-

ilarly involves three things: the cheater, his action, and the rules of the game.) I leave aside for the moment the question (in the end, perhaps exceedingly important) of whether we should in fact include a fourth element in the complex: the person spoken to, the other player. Some might well wish, as I do, to add a fifth: the transcendent dimension—of truth, fairness, and such. The common view that the truth of a statement is a function of the relation between it and the overt facts may be termed a bilateral conception.

4. *Qawm kānū ṣadaqū bi-alsinatihim, wa-lam yuṣaddiqū qawlahum bi-fi'lihim.* Literally: 'A people who used to give *ṣidq* with their tongues, but did not give *taṣdīq* to what they said by their action.' Abū Ja'far Muḥammad ibn Jarīr al-Ṭabarī, *Jāmi' al-Bayān fī Tafsīr al-Qur'ān*, ad 49:14.

5. The Islamic epistemological point that Muslims learn what the final truth is about man's duty and destiny through the divine disclosure of it (in their case, in the Qur'ān) was of course taken for granted in the theological treatises, and eventually colours the further discussion of faith a little, though surprisingly little. As my presentation has perhaps made clear and as I document in *Faith and Belief*, pp. [33]–52, a sizeable portion of many passages in Islamic theology about faith could be introduced word for word in Christian discussions of the matter almost without modification, and with considerable profit. And the same might be true to some degree, in humanist discussions.

Originally the intention was that this present paper was to have been entitled 'Where Lies Religious Truth?' and was to develop specifically the view that the locus of *religious* truth is persons. The argument would have elaborated the consideration of the *taṣdīq* conceptualization, for the Islamic case, and would have endeavoured to systematize theoretically the personalist-truth notions set forth in my recent work *Questions of Religious Truth*. In tackling this, however, I found myself increasingly disquieted by the notion that any truth about us humans, whether religious or other, can be localized in a proposition; and I found myself writing instead this present, less satisfactory but I suppose more provocative, paper. Perhaps a sober position might finally be that truth or falsity, in this realm, is a function not of a proposition only but of it and of the person who makes it, but that there is perhaps a range of types of proposition, with the personalist element being lowest (or merely most universal?) when the proposition refers to natural science matters, higher when it refers to social science matters, very high in various special cases, and highest in the religious realm. For another day, perhaps.

6. I am not arguing here that with the propositional-truth notion one cannot cope with personalisms as a special case—just as I trust that my

critics will not suppose that with the personalist view being proposed it would be impossible to accommodate, again as a rather special case, certain impersonal objectivisms. The question is rather one of where one puts primacy. And especially, of where one puts aspiration—not merely individually but socially, institutionally (as we consider below about Harvard's aspiration).

With the diffidence of an outsider in these matters, I venture to ponder some of Austin's handling of this particular issue in my next note.

7. An outsider such as I to philosophy as a modern academic discipline dare not but be tentative and diffident in these matters; I dare venture into this area at all only because I see the issues as not strictly within philosophy—at least, not philosophy as contemporarily understood—but rather as having to do with the relation between philosophy and culture, and that between culture and human life (understood historically, but in a way transcending Western, and especially modern Western, particularities, for those who wish to remain empirical; understood in ultimate or absolute or religious terms, for those who allow these).

First, then, is it fanciful to raise a perhaps innocent inquiry regarding Wittgenstein's famous problem of games? The philosopher may ask what all those things called 'game' have in common, and find nothing; may press one's modern fellows to search and scrutinize and *look* at games to see what indeed they have in common; may be perhaps a whit disparaging when, although they cannot find such a thing objectively there, they yet continue to feel uneasily that 'they must have something in common because we call them all games'. Might he have missed something at once both simple and important? He is suggesting that we should look at games to see what is common in them, or whether indeed anything is; I suggest that we look rather at persons playing games, and see what the various instances have in common. What characterizes them all, despite their diversity, is that we human beings are related to them in a particular way. Moderns do not see it because they are looking in the wrong place. The ruthless insistence that the proper way, the only way, to understand the world is to see it apart from human relations to it, may not be so legitimate as some have thought. This principle of 'objectivity' may lead, or have led, to something reasonably called truth in the natural sciences, but I ponder the possibility that it may lead to error in the 'behavioural' sciences and in all our apprehension of things that pertain to the human. On another occasion I have defined 'objectivity' as the proper way to handle objects intellectually; but to treat men, women and children, or anything involving them, as if they were objects is to misunderstand them.

Might one propose: Nothing that humans do can be adequately understood objectively?

Might one further raise a question also about Austin, and even perhaps speculate whether his views do not in some fashion lend surreptitious support to such a proposal? Although here again I feel highly diffident in exposing my uncouthness in the unfamiliar field of modern philosophy, I venture to trespass in that field if only to profit from expert comment. An outsider's questions may sound inept, but through them the questioner, at least, may win some light. With regard to Austin's essay 'Truth', my unsophisticated feeling is that he comes close to being a moralist and personalist, but would shy away from formulating his position so. His notion of 'statement', for example (as distinct from a sentence), which seems certainly non-empirical, non-'objective', appears strikingly supernatural unless it be interpreted as an implicitly personalist conception. Indeed it is of something said 'by a certain person' (p. 87), and when two persons use the same sentence it may make two statements, one for each (p. 88). Moreover he was clearly fascinated with promises, and stressed the moral-personal dimension even of knowing (e.g., in 'Other Minds'). On some points, however, he was unwilling to be personalist: for example for him 'that cat may be on the mat' (I prefer 'I love you' as a paradigm for truth or falsity!) 'is not a statement' and cannot be true or false (p. 100); is it, however, unreasonable much to prefer the Arabic dictionaries' notion that when one says something of that kind, one may be lying or may be telling the truth?

Moreover, an outsider wonders whether Austin is being perhaps a trifle facile when he tosses off the point that the sentence 'It is mine' may make different statements, depending on who utters it. He does not seem to be concerned with how profoundly personalist he is thereby constituting his concept of 'statement' to be. Whether 'It is mine' is true or false depends *both* on who says it, *and* on certain objective matters. It seems worth pondering whether religious pronouncements are not of this kind (and, I am even suggesting, perhaps in the end all pronouncements). Some thinkers, having discovered that religious sentences (and in this they are like more conspicuously personal sentences, such as 'I am twenty years old') are not true or false in themselves, considered objectively, have gone on to assert that they are then meaningless—or that they merely express emotions. Now the sentence 'I am twenty years old' is, I suppose, strictly meaningless, considered in and of itself (also: 'He is twenty years old'). It becomes a meaningful statement when considered in relation to particular persons; the truth of it, however, still depends on its relation, then, to matters in the objective, empirical world. (Without developing the point, I think that it could be argued that even scientific statements are meaningless in and of themselves; their truth comes into significance when related to persons, but in their case the persons are not *particular* persons but all humankind, in theory; but in fact, provided that they understand the language being used.) Religious formulations, so far as I can see, are perhaps analogous, in relation not so strictly to particular individuals, although that remains, but first to communities. In the course of teaching Islamic and Hindu ideas, I have had the experience of observing how they seem at first 'meaningless' to outsiders; although it is obviously absurd to judge meaningless simply what one cannot understand. References: Ludwig Wittgenstein, *Philosophische Untersuchungen/Philosophical Investigations*, para 66. [p. 31: I have not followed exactly the English translation p. 31e]; J. L. Austin, *Philosophical Papers*, 'Other Minds' pp. 44–84, 'Truth' pp. 85–101.

8. This point, so far as religious formulations are concerned (and specifically the proposition 'The Qur'ān is the word of God'), is explored in my *Questions of Religious Truth*.

9. Neither would it be false. (A statement is not considered a lie, even if the person who makes it does so without believing it—or even with intent to deceive—if the content of the statement happens nonetheless to be correct.) Curiously, a journal article that is not true, in the above sense, for the author, may yet become true for certain readers if it both states facts correctly and becomes incorporated with integrity into a given reader's life and personality.

To my astonishment, this particular paragraph in the text aroused, in preliminary discussions (though not at the conference on the philosophy of religion at the University of Birmingham, in April 1970 [chaired by John Hick] where this paper was originally delivered), the most acute resistance of anything in the entire thesis. In fact, several colleagues pleaded with me to withdraw it. I was surprised at this reaction, since I had imagined that almost everyone feels that we must do something to curtail the 'publish or perish' stance that is helping to vitiate modern academic life, and that falls so burdensomely especially on the young; and must do something too to curtail the sheer amount of academic publication, some of it trivial, with which we are inundated. Surely it is not too heretical to suggest that a society is sinful that talks (and encourages talking) in order to be heard. Should we not aim at a society, or at least at a university community, that has the sincerity to talk, or at least to value talking, only when it has something to say, something it feels is worth saying? Most academics recognize intellectually and feel emotionally the sorry inhumanity of modern commercial advertising in its unctuous insincerity, but sometimes we are insensitive to the academic advertising that can colour our learned societies and our journals. The graduating medical student takes an oath to use his skill only for the welfare of humankind; some sort of counterpart to the Hippocratic oath for the humanities would pledge us never to publish an article primarily for our own advantage. (Rumour has it that in the natural sciences also a good deal of research nowadays is competitive, not disinterested.) At the very least, we should recognize that we are all sinners. At the very, very least, we should recognize that it is not easy to speak the truth. It is not the case that science and the objective method have made available to us a path to truth that by-passes personal morality, that by-passes persons.

10. This introduces the fourth component in what would become, then, a quadrilateral relationship in which truth is involved; see note 3, above.

11. Relevant to the last two considerations is the concept of 'discipline'. This is not precisely defined, and there are a few aspects of the notion that are perhaps valuable, and could be salvaged. Yet one of the questions that I find myself asking—and I am not unaware that this is bold—is whether in general this concept, increasingly dominant in Western intellectual life, has not with its concomitants constituted a formidable disruption. It has largely replaced 'subject-matter' as the operative conception in much university study; and particularly perhaps in the United States it ramifies into and controls a frighteningly large part of what a university does and how it does it. I realize, accordingly, that to question it may appear not merely radical but ridiculous, inane. I do so, however, seriously and responsibly. I have come deeply to feel that the transition from 'subject' to 'discipline' may have constituted a major step in that profoundly wrong turn that has been taken by Western intellectual life somewhere along the line, in the course of the last many decades. Again, this concept may be legitimate in the natural sciences, but in the study of human affairs it is, I think that I discern, intellectually an error. To write only for one's peers in a discipline is to write not only jargon but—in principle—falsehood; or at least, not truth.

12. In this case the personal morality might be not simply or perhaps even primarily the personal integrity in relation to his or her work of the individual researcher (although that would be interesting to discuss) but, given the universalist quality of scientific statements, rather or also the group morality of humankind.

13. *Tawḥīd*, to use another Islamic term.

CHAPTER 8. OBJECTIVITY AND THE HUMANE SCIENCES: A NEW PROPOSAL

1. Gregory Baum, 'Objectivity and the Social Sciences'; read at the annual meetings of the Canadian Society for the Study of Religion, May, 1974, Toronto.

2. James Mallory, 'Responsive and Responsible Government', published (as was this present article) in *Transactions of the Royal Society of Canada*, IV, vol. xii, 1974.

WORKS CITED

Thomas Aquinas. *Liber de Veritate Catholicae Fidei contra errores Infidelium, qui dicitur Summa Contra Gentiles*, ed. Cesla[us] Pera, D. Petr[us] Marc, et al. 3 vols. Augustae Taurinorum: Marietti, 1961–7; English translations: *On the Truth of the Catholic Faith: Summa Contra Gentiles, translated, with an Introduction and Notes*, by Anton C. Pegis et al. 5 vols. Garden City, New York: Doubleday (Image Books), 1955–7; and Joseph Rickaby, S.J. *Of God and His Creatures: an annotated translation (with some abridgement) of the Summa contra Gentiles of Saint Thos Aquinas*. St. Louis: Herder, and London: Burns & Oates, 1905

Thomas Aquinas. *Quaestiones Disputatae*, vol. I: *De Veritate*, ed. Raymund[us] Spiazzi. Taurini, Romae: Marietti, 1964; English translation: *Truth*, trans. by James B. McGlynn. 3 vols. Chicago: Henry Regner, 1952–4

Thomas Aquinas. *Summa Theologiae*. Turin and Rome: Marietti, 1926

J.L. Austin. *Philosophical Papers*. Oxford: Clarendon Press 1961

Werner Cohn. 'What is Religion? An Analysis for Cross-Cultural Comparisions', *Journal of Christian Education*, 7 (1964), [116]–138

Werner Cohn. '"Religion", in Non-Western Countries', *American Anthropologist*, 69 (1967), 73–76

Werner Cohn. 'On the Problem of Religion in Non-Western Cultures', *Internationales Jahrbuch für Religionssociologie / International Yearbook for the Sociology of Religion*, 5 (1969), [7]–19

G.-Ed. Demers. 'Les divers sens du mot 'ratio' au moyen âge', in *Études d' histoire littéraire et doctrinale du XIIIᵉ siècle*, Première Série. Publications de l'Institut d'Etudes Médiévales d'Ottawa. Paris: Vrin, and Ottawa: Inst. d'Études Médiévales, 1932 [105]–139

Michel Despland. *La Religion en Occident: évolution des idées et du vécu*. Coll. 'Héritage et Projet', #23. Montreal: Fides, 1979

Émile Durkheim. *Les formes élémentaires de la vie religieuse: Le système totémique en Australie.* Bibliothèque de philosophie contemporaine. 1st ed. Paris: Felix Arcan, 1912; English translation by Joseph Ward Swain. *The Elementary Forms of the Religious Life: a study in religious sociology.* London: Allen & Unwin, and New York: Macmillan, [1915]

A.J. Festugière. *Épicure et ses dieux.* Coll. 'Mythes et Religions'. Paris: Presses Universitaires de France, 1946

W.K.C. Guthrie. *A History of Greek Philosophy.* Vol. III. Cambridge: Cambridge University Press, 1969

Werner Jaeger. 'Über Ursprung und Kreislauf des philosophischen Lebensideals', in *Sitzungsberichte der preussischen Akademie der Wissenschaften—Jahrgang 1928: Philosophisch-historische Klasse.* Berlin: Verlag der Akademie der Wissenschaften/Walter de Gruyter 1928, 390–421

Werner Jaeger. *Aristotle: Fundamentals of the History of his Development,* Richard Robinson, trans. Oxford: Clarendon Press, [1934] 1948

Werner Jaeger. *Humanism and Theology.* The Aquinas Lecture. Milwaukee: Marquette University Press, 1943

Immanuel Kant. *Die Religion innerhalb der Grenzen der blossen Vernunft.* Königsberg: Friedrich Nicolovius, 1793

Thomas Kuhn. *The Structure of Scientific Revolutions.* Chicago: Chicago University Press, 1962 and 1969

A.D. Nock. *Conversion: The Old and the New in Religion from Alexander the Great to Augustine of Hippo.* London &c.: Oxford University Press, [1933] 1963

Theodore Roszak. *The Making of a Counter Culture: Reflections on the Technocratic Society and its Youthful Opposition.* New York: Doubleday, 1969

F.S.C. Schiller. *Humanism: philosophical essays.* London: Macmillan, 1903

Friedrich Schleiermacher. *Der christliche Glaube: nach den Grundsätzen der evangelischen Kirche im Zusammenhange dargestellt.* Zweite umbearbeitete Ausgabe. 2 vols. Berlin: G. Reimer, 1830; Martin Redeker edition. 2 vols. Berlin: de Gruyter, 1960; English trans. edited by H.R. Mackintosh and J.S. Stewart. *The Christian Faith.* Edinburgh: T. & T. Clark, 1928

Friedrich Schleiermacher. *Über die Religion: Reden an die Gebildeten unter ihren Verächtern*. Berlin: Johann Friedrich Unger, 1799; 2nd revised edition. Berlin: Reimer, 1806; English translation: *On Religion: speeches to its cultured despisers. Translated from the 3rd edition, with introduction*, by John Oman. London: Kegan Paul, Trench, Trübner, 1893

Wilfred Cantwell Smith. *Belief and History*. Richard Lectures for 1974–75, University of Virginia. Charlottesville: University Press of Virginia, 1977 & 1985

Wilfred Cantwell Smith. *Faith and Belief*. Princeton: Princeton University Press, 1979 & 1987

Wilfred Cantwell Smith. *The Meaning and End of Religion*. New York: Macmillan, 1963; Most recent edition, Minneapolis: Fortress, and London: SCM, 1991

Wilfred Cantwell Smith. 'Religion as Symbolism', Introduction to *Propaedia*, part 8, 'Religion'. *The New Encyclopaedia Britannica*. 15th ed. 1974, vol. 1, 498–500

Wilfred Cantwell Smith. *Questions of Religious Truth*. New York: Scribners and London: Gollancz, 1967

Wilfred Cantwell Smith. *Towards a World Theology: Faith and the Comparative History of Religion*. London: Macmillan, and Philadelphia: Westminster, 1981

Wilfred Cantwell Smith. 'Traditional Religion and Modern Culture', in *Proceedings of the XIth International Congress of the International Association for the History of Religions . . . at Claremont, California, September 6–11, 1965*. Leiden: E.J. Brill, 1968, vol. 1

Arthur Waley. *Three Ways of Thought in Ancient China*. London: Allen & Unwin, [1939] 1974

Ludwig Wittgenstein. *Philosophische Untersuchungen/Philosophical Investigations*. Trans. G.E.M. Anscombe. Oxford: Basil Blackwell 1967

INDEX

'Abd Al-Rahman, 86
Abelard, 59
Anglican: view of truth, 26
Aquinas, St. Thomas, 54–57,
150–52
Austin, J., 163

Barth, K., 155–56
Baum, G., 165
Belief, 25, 74
Besant, A., 148
Buber, M., 158
Buddha: 'fearlessness pose', 3–4, 6
Buddhist: as understood by the
West, 24–25, 27–28; faith, 6,
32; missionary movement, 29

Catholic, 54, 56
Chinese religion, 5, 29
Christian: church, 28; doctrine,
16, 25–26, 36; faith, 6, 61–63;
history and science, 9–10;
theology, 59, 94; thought, 58
Clement of Alexandria, 148
Cohn, W., 20–21, 147
Community, 138, 143–44
Comparing: cultures, vii–ix, 9–10,
19, 99, 109, 126–27, 139;
religious traditions, 17, 20–21,
23, 27–28, 31, 41–42, 75–76,
132, 144
Comte, A., 148
Concept: as symbol, 4–5; God as,
5; need for revision, 78–79;
conceptualization, 29, 112
'Confucianism', 44–45, 73

Dance: central organizing
principle, 26
Deception, 103–4
Despland, M., 147, 153
Druze, 28
Durkheim, É., 52–54, 149–50

Elementary: as translation of
French, 52–53, 150

Faith, viii–ix, 7, 9, 16–17, 33–34,
40, 107–8, 132–33, 155, 161;
as generic noun, 54–56, 60–62,
156–57; cohesive yet
destructive, 7; how understood,
133; in liberal values, 90; in
reason, 43, 45–46; in science,
45; intersection of eternity and
human, 17; loss of, 43;
translation of German, 61–63,
156–59
Fascism, 97
Festugière, A. J., 20, 147
Fundamentalism, 95

God, 5, 9, 15–17, 57, 101, 108;
concept of, 5, 39
Graeco-Roman tradition, 159–60;
as religion, 19–21, 35–36, 41,
48, 67–69, 79–81, 93

Hegel, G. W. F., 47, 153
Hindu: philosophy, 44–45;
religion, 30
History: and religion, 15–16; and
science, 10–15; as process, 85;